C-1674    CAREER EXAMINATION SERIES

*This is your PASSBOOK for...*

# Structure Maintainer Trainee, Group E (Plumbing)

*Test Preparation Study Guide
Questions & Answers*

# COPYRIGHT NOTICE

This book is SOLELY intended for, is sold ONLY to, and its use is RESTRICTED to individual, bona fide applicants or candidates who qualify by virtue of having seriously filed applications for appropriate license, certificate, professional and/or promotional advancement, higher school matriculation, scholarship, or other legitimate requirements of education and/or governmental authorities.

This book is NOT intended for use, class instruction, tutoring, training, duplication, copying, reprinting, excerption, or adaptation, etc., by:

1) Other publishers
2) Proprietors and/or Instructors of "Coaching" and/or Preparatory Courses
3) Personnel and/or Training Divisions of commercial, industrial, and governmental organizations
4) Schools, colleges, or universities and/or their departments and staffs, including teachers and other personnel
5) Testing Agencies or Bureaus
6) Study groups which seek by the purchase of a single volume to copy and/or duplicate and/or adapt this material for use by the group as a whole without having purchased individual volumes for each of the members of the group
7) Et al.

Such persons would be in violation of appropriate Federal and State statutes.

PROVISION OF LICENSING AGREEMENTS – Recognized educational, commercial, industrial, and governmental institutions and organizations, and others legitimately engaged in educational pursuits, including training, testing, and measurement activities, may address request for a licensing agreement to the copyright owners, who will determine whether, and under what conditions, including fees and charges, the materials in this book may be used them. In other words, a licensing facility exists for the legitimate use of the material in this book on other than an individual basis. However, it is asseverated and affirmed here that the material in this book CANNOT be used without the receipt of the express permission of such a licensing agreement from the Publishers. Inquiries re licensing should be addressed to the company, attention rights and permissions department.

All rights reserved, including the right of reproduction in whole or in part, in any form or by any means, electronic or mechanical, including photocopying, recording, or by any information storage and retrieval system, without permission in writing from the Publisher.

Copyright © 2025 by
## National Learning Corporation

212 Michael Drive, Syosset, NY 11791
(516) 921-8888 • www.passbooks.com
E-mail: info@passbooks.com

# PASSBOOK® SERIES

THE *PASSBOOK® SERIES* has been created to prepare applicants and candidates for the ultimate academic battlefield – the examination room.

At some time in our lives, each and every one of us may be required to take an examination – for validation, matriculation, admission, qualification, registration, certification, or licensure.

Based on the assumption that every applicant or candidate has met the basic formal educational standards, has taken the required number of courses, and read the necessary texts, the *PASSBOOK® SERIES* furnishes the one special preparation which may assure passing with confidence, instead of failing with insecurity. Examination questions – together with answers – are furnished as the basic vehicle for study so that the mysteries of the examination and its compounding difficulties may be eliminated or diminished by a sure method.

This book is meant to help you pass your examination provided that you qualify and are serious in your objective.

The entire field is reviewed through the huge store of content information which is succinctly presented through a provocative and challenging approach – the question-and-answer method.

A climate of success is established by furnishing the correct answers at the end of each test.

You soon learn to recognize types of questions, forms of questions, and patterns of questioning. You may even begin to anticipate expected outcomes.

You perceive that many questions are repeated or adapted so that you can gain acute insights, which may enable you to score many sure points.

You learn how to confront new questions, or types of questions, and to attack them confidently and work out the correct answers.

You note objectives and emphases, and recognize pitfalls and dangers, so that you may make positive educational adjustments.

Moreover, you are kept fully informed in relation to new concepts, methods, practices, and directions in the field.

You discover that you are actually taking the examination all the time: you are preparing for the examination by "taking" an examination, not by reading extraneous and/or supererogatory textbooks.

In short, this PASSBOOK®, used directedly, should be an important factor in helping you to pass your test.

# STRUCTURE MAINTAINER TRAINEE—GROUP E

JOB DESCRIPTION:
Under close supervision, receives a course of training in plumbing work on subway, elevated and surface structures, including stations, enclosures and related buildings. Assists Structure Maintainers—Group E. Performs such other duties as the Transit Authority is authorized by law to prescribe in its regulations

EXAMPLES OF TYPICAL TASKS:
Assists and is trained in the installation, maintenance and repair of plumbing fixtures in toilets and sink rooms, and heating, water and drainage systems. Is trained to clean, test, and repair pipes, fixtures, vents and hot water heaters. Does incidental painting. Loads, unloads and drives motor vehicles.

TEST DESCRIPTION:
The multiple-choice test may include questions on: fundamentals of the plumbing trade, including the proper selection, use and care of tools, materials and equipment used in plumbing work; reading and understanding technical drawings; performing job-related arithmetic; safe work practices, including basic first-aid procedures; and other related areas.

# HOW TO TAKE A TEST

I. YOU MUST PASS AN EXAMINATION

A. *WHAT EVERY CANDIDATE SHOULD KNOW*

Examination applicants often ask us for help in preparing for the written test. What can I study in advance? What kinds of questions will be asked? How will the test be given? How will the papers be graded?

As an applicant for a civil service examination, you may be wondering about some of these things. Our purpose here is to suggest effective methods of advance study and to describe civil service examinations.

Your chances for success on this examination can be increased if you know how to prepare. Those "pre-examination jitters" can be reduced if you know what to expect. You can even experience an adventure in good citizenship if you know why civil service exams are given.

B. *WHY ARE CIVIL SERVICE EXAMINATIONS GIVEN?*

Civil service examinations are important to you in two ways. As a citizen, you want public jobs filled by employees who know how to do their work. As a job seeker, you want a fair chance to compete for that job on an equal footing with other candidates. The best-known means of accomplishing this two-fold goal is the competitive examination.

Exams are widely publicized throughout the nation. They may be administered for jobs in federal, state, city, municipal, town or village governments or agencies.

Any citizen may apply, with some limitations, such as the age or residence of applicants. Your experience and education may be reviewed to see whether you meet the requirements for the particular examination. When these requirements exist, they are reasonable and applied consistently to all applicants. Thus, a competitive examination may cause you some uneasiness now, but it is your privilege and safeguard.

C. *HOW ARE CIVIL SERVICE EXAMS DEVELOPED?*

Examinations are carefully written by trained technicians who are specialists in the field known as "psychological measurement," in consultation with recognized authorities in the field of work that the test will cover. These experts recommend the subject matter areas or skills to be tested; only those knowledges or skills important to your success on the job are included. The most reliable books and source materials available are used as references. Together, the experts and technicians judge the difficulty level of the questions.

Test technicians know how to phrase questions so that the problem is clearly stated. Their ethics do not permit "trick" or "catch" questions. Questions may have been tried out on sample groups, or subjected to statistical analysis, to determine their usefulness.

Written tests are often used in combination with performance tests, ratings of training and experience, and oral interviews. All of these measures combine to form the best-known means of finding the right person for the right job.

## II. HOW TO PASS THE WRITTEN TEST

### A. NATURE OF THE EXAMINATION

To prepare intelligently for civil service examinations, you should know how they differ from school examinations you have taken. In school you were assigned certain definite pages to read or subjects to cover. The examination questions were quite detailed and usually emphasized memory. Civil service exams, on the other hand, try to discover your present ability to perform the duties of a position, plus your potentiality to learn these duties. In other words, a civil service exam attempts to predict how successful you will be. Questions cover such a broad area that they cannot be as minute and detailed as school exam questions.

In the public service similar kinds of work, or positions, are grouped together in one "class." This process is known as *position-classification*. All the positions in a class are paid according to the salary range for that class. One class title covers all of these positions, and they are all tested by the same examination.

### B. FOUR BASIC STEPS

#### 1) Study the announcement

How, then, can you know what subjects to study? Our best answer is: "Learn as much as possible about the class of positions for which you've applied." The exam will test the knowledge, skills and abilities needed to do the work.

Your most valuable source of information about the position you want is the official exam announcement. This announcement lists the training and experience qualifications. Check these standards and apply only if you come reasonably close to meeting them.

The brief description of the position in the examination announcement offers some clues to the subjects which will be tested. Think about the job itself. Review the duties in your mind. Can you perform them, or are there some in which you are rusty? Fill in the blank spots in your preparation.

Many jurisdictions preview the written test in the exam announcement by including a section called "Knowledge and Abilities Required," "Scope of the Examination," or some similar heading. Here you will find out specifically what fields will be tested.

#### 2) Review your own background

Once you learn in general what the position is all about, and what you need to know to do the work, ask yourself which subjects you already know fairly well and which need improvement. You may wonder whether to concentrate on improving your strong areas or on building some background in your fields of weakness. When the announcement has specified "some knowledge" or "considerable knowledge," or has used adjectives like "beginning principles of…" or "advanced … methods," you can get a clue as to the number and difficulty of questions to be asked in any given field. More questions, and hence broader coverage, would be included for those subjects which are more important in the work. Now weigh your strengths and weaknesses against the job requirements and prepare accordingly.

#### 3) Determine the level of the position

Another way to tell how intensively you should prepare is to understand the level of the job for which you are applying. Is it the entering level? In other words, is this the position in which beginners in a field of work are hired? Or is it an intermediate or advanced level? Sometimes this is indicated by such words as "Junior" or "Senior" in the class title. Other jurisdictions use Roman numerals to designate the level – Clerk I, Clerk II, for example. The word "Supervisor" sometimes appears in the title. If the level is not indicated by the title, check the description of duties. Will you be working under very close supervision, or will you have responsibility for independent decisions in this work?

**4) Choose appropriate study materials**

Now that you know the subjects to be examined and the relative amount of each subject to be covered, you can choose suitable study materials. For beginning level jobs, or even advanced ones, if you have a pronounced weakness in some aspect of your training, read a modern, standard textbook in that field. Be sure it is up to date and has general coverage. Such books are normally available at your library, and the librarian will be glad to help you locate one. For entry-level positions, questions of appropriate difficulty are chosen – neither highly advanced questions, nor those too simple. Such questions require careful thought but not advanced training.

If the position for which you are applying is technical or advanced, you will read more advanced, specialized material. If you are already familiar with the basic principles of your field, elementary textbooks would waste your time. Concentrate on advanced textbooks and technical periodicals. Think through the concepts and review difficult problems in your field.

These are all general sources. You can get more ideas on your own initiative, following these leads. For example, training manuals and publications of the government agency which employs workers in your field can be useful, particularly for technical and professional positions. A letter or visit to the government department involved may result in more specific study suggestions, and certainly will provide you with a more definite idea of the exact nature of the position you are seeking.

## III. KINDS OF TESTS

Tests are used for purposes other than measuring knowledge and ability to perform specified duties. For some positions, it is equally important to test ability to make adjustments to new situations or to profit from training. In others, basic mental abilities not dependent on information are essential. Questions which test these things may not appear as pertinent to the duties of the position as those which test for knowledge and information. Yet they are often highly important parts of a fair examination. For very general questions, it is almost impossible to help you direct your study efforts. What we can do is to point out some of the more common of these general abilities needed in public service positions and describe some typical questions.

1) General information

Broad, general information has been found useful for predicting job success in some kinds of work. This is tested in a variety of ways, from vocabulary lists to questions about current events. Basic background in some field of work, such as sociology or economics, may be sampled in a group of questions. Often these are principles which have become familiar to most persons through exposure rather than through formal training. It is difficult to advise you how to study for these questions; being alert to the world around you is our best suggestion.

2) Verbal ability

An example of an ability needed in many positions is verbal or language ability. Verbal ability is, in brief, the ability to use and understand words. Vocabulary and grammar tests are typical measures of this ability. Reading comprehension or paragraph interpretation questions are common in many kinds of civil service tests. You are given a paragraph of written material and asked to find its central meaning.

3) Numerical ability
Number skills can be tested by the familiar arithmetic problem, by checking paired lists of numbers to see which are alike and which are different, or by interpreting charts and graphs. In the latter test, a graph may be printed in the test booklet which you are asked to use as the basis for answering questions.

4) Observation
A popular test for law-enforcement positions is the observation test. A picture is shown to you for several minutes, then taken away. Questions about the picture test your ability to observe both details and larger elements.

5) Following directions
In many positions in the public service, the employee must be able to carry out written instructions dependably and accurately. You may be given a chart with several columns, each column listing a variety of information. The questions require you to carry out directions involving the information given in the chart.

6) Skills and aptitudes
Performance tests effectively measure some manual skills and aptitudes. When the skill is one in which you are trained, such as typing or shorthand, you can practice. These tests are often very much like those given in business school or high school courses. For many of the other skills and aptitudes, however, no short-time preparation can be made. Skills and abilities natural to you or that you have developed throughout your lifetime are being tested.

Many of the general questions just described provide all the data needed to answer the questions and ask you to use your reasoning ability to find the answers. Your best preparation for these tests, as well as for tests of facts and ideas, is to be at your physical and mental best. You, no doubt, have your own methods of getting into an exam-taking mood and keeping "in shape." The next section lists some ideas on this subject.

## IV. KINDS OF QUESTIONS

Only rarely is the "essay" question, which you answer in narrative form, used in civil service tests. Civil service tests are usually of the short-answer type. Full instructions for answering these questions will be given to you at the examination. But in case this is your first experience with short-answer questions and separate answer sheets, here is what you need to know:

### 1) Multiple-choice Questions
Most popular of the short-answer questions is the "multiple choice" or "best answer" question. It can be used, for example, to test for factual knowledge, ability to solve problems or judgment in meeting situations found at work.

A multiple-choice question is normally one of three types—
- It can begin with an incomplete statement followed by several possible endings. You are to find the one ending which *best* completes the statement, although some of the others may not be entirely wrong.
- It can also be a complete statement in the form of a question which is answered by choosing one of the statements listed.

- It can be in the form of a problem – again you select the best answer.

Here is an example of a multiple-choice question with a discussion which should give you some clues as to the method for choosing the right answer:

When an employee has a complaint about his assignment, the action which will *best* help him overcome his difficulty is to
- A. discuss his difficulty with his coworkers
- B. take the problem to the head of the organization
- C. take the problem to the person who gave him the assignment
- D. say nothing to anyone about his complaint

In answering this question, you should study each of the choices to find which is best. Consider choice "A" – Certainly an employee may discuss his complaint with fellow employees, but no change or improvement can result, and the complaint remains unresolved. Choice "B" is a poor choice since the head of the organization probably does not know what assignment you have been given, and taking your problem to him is known as "going over the head" of the supervisor. The supervisor, or person who made the assignment, is the person who can clarify it or correct any injustice. Choice "C" is, therefore, correct. To say nothing, as in choice "D," is unwise. Supervisors have and interest in knowing the problems employees are facing, and the employee is seeking a solution to his problem.

## 2) True/False Questions

The "true/false" or "right/wrong" form of question is sometimes used. Here a complete statement is given. Your job is to decide whether the statement is right or wrong.

SAMPLE: A roaming cell-phone call to a nearby city costs less than a non-roaming call to a distant city.

This statement is wrong, or false, since roaming calls are more expensive.

This is not a complete list of all possible question forms, although most of the others are variations of these common types. You will always get complete directions for answering questions. Be sure you understand *how* to mark your answers – ask questions until you do.

## V. RECORDING YOUR ANSWERS

Computer terminals are used more and more today for many different kinds of exams.

For an examination with very few applicants, you may be told to record your answers in the test booklet itself. Separate answer sheets are much more common. If this separate answer sheet is to be scored by machine – and this is often the case – it is highly important that you mark your answers correctly in order to get credit.

An electronic scoring machine is often used in civil service offices because of the speed with which papers can be scored. Machine-scored answer sheets must be marked with a pencil, which will be given to you. This pencil has a high graphite content which responds to the electronic scoring machine. As a matter of fact, stray dots may register as answers, so do not let your pencil rest on the answer sheet while you are pondering the correct answer. Also, if your pencil lead breaks or is otherwise defective, ask for another.

Since the answer sheet will be dropped in a slot in the scoring machine, be careful not to bend the corners or get the paper crumpled.

The answer sheet normally has five vertical columns of numbers, with 30 numbers to a column. These numbers correspond to the question numbers in your test booklet. After each number, going across the page are four or five pairs of dotted lines. These short dotted lines have small letters or numbers above them. The first two pairs may also have a "T" or "F" above the letters. This indicates that the first two pairs only are to be used if the questions are of the true-false type. If the questions are multiple choice, disregard the "T" and "F" and pay attention only to the small letters or numbers.

Answer your questions in the manner of the sample that follows:

32. The largest city in the United States is
   A. Washington, D.C.
   B. New York City
   C. Chicago
   D. Detroit
   E. San Francisco

1) Choose the answer you think is best. (New York City is the largest, so "B" is correct.)
2) Find the row of dotted lines numbered the same as the question you are answering. (Find row number 32)
3) Find the pair of dotted lines corresponding to the answer. (Find the pair of lines under the mark "B.")
4) Make a solid black mark between the dotted lines.


## VI. BEFORE THE TEST

Common sense will help you find procedures to follow to get ready for an examination. Too many of us, however, overlook these sensible measures. Indeed, nervousness and fatigue have been found to be the most serious reasons why applicants fail to do their best on civil service tests. Here is a list of reminders:

- Begin your preparation early – Don't wait until the last minute to go scurrying around for books and materials or to find out what the position is all about.
- Prepare continuously – An hour a night for a week is better than an all-night cram session. This has been definitely established. What is more, a night a week for a month will return better dividends than crowding your study into a shorter period of time.
- Locate the place of the exam – You have been sent a notice telling you when and where to report for the examination. If the location is in a different town or otherwise unfamiliar to you, it would be well to inquire the best route and learn something about the building.
- Relax the night before the test – Allow your mind to rest. Do not study at all that night. Plan some mild recreation or diversion; then go to bed early and get a good night's sleep.
- Get up early enough to make a leisurely trip to the place for the test – This way unforeseen events, traffic snarls, unfamiliar buildings, etc. will not upset you.
- Dress comfortably – A written test is not a fashion show. You will be known by number and not by name, so wear something comfortable.

- Leave excess paraphernalia at home – Shopping bags and odd bundles will get in your way. You need bring only the items mentioned in the official notice you received; usually everything you need is provided. Do not bring reference books to the exam. They will only confuse those last minutes and be taken away from you when in the test room.
- Arrive somewhat ahead of time – If because of transportation schedules you must get there very early, bring a newspaper or magazine to take your mind off yourself while waiting.
- Locate the examination room – When you have found the proper room, you will be directed to the seat or part of the room where you will sit. Sometimes you are given a sheet of instructions to read while you are waiting. Do not fill out any forms until you are told to do so; just read them and be prepared.
- Relax and prepare to listen to the instructions
- If you have any physical problem that may keep you from doing your best, be sure to tell the test administrator. If you are sick or in poor health, you really cannot do your best on the exam. You can come back and take the test some other time.

## VII. AT THE TEST

The day of the test is here and you have the test booklet in your hand. The temptation to get going is very strong. Caution! There is more to success than knowing the right answers. You must know how to identify your papers and understand variations in the type of short-answer question used in this particular examination. Follow these suggestions for maximum results from your efforts:

### 1) Cooperate with the monitor

The test administrator has a duty to create a situation in which you can be as much at ease as possible. He will give instructions, tell you when to begin, check to see that you are marking your answer sheet correctly, and so on. He is not there to guard you, although he will see that your competitors do not take unfair advantage. He wants to help you do your best.

### 2) Listen to all instructions

Don't jump the gun! Wait until you understand all directions. In most civil service tests you get more time than you need to answer the questions. So don't be in a hurry. Read each word of instructions until you clearly understand the meaning. Study the examples, listen to all announcements and follow directions. Ask questions if you do not understand what to do.

### 3) Identify your papers

Civil service exams are usually identified by number only. You will be assigned a number; you must not put your name on your test papers. Be sure to copy your number correctly. Since more than one exam may be given, copy your exact examination title.

### 4) Plan your time

Unless you are told that a test is a "speed" or "rate of work" test, speed itself is usually not important. Time enough to answer all the questions will be provided, but this does not mean that you have all day. An overall time limit has been set. Divide the total time (in minutes) by the number of questions to determine the approximate time you have for each question.

**5) Do not linger over difficult questions**

If you come across a difficult question, mark it with a paper clip (useful to have along) and come back to it when you have been through the booklet. One caution if you do this – be sure to skip a number on your answer sheet as well. Check often to be sure that you have not lost your place and that you are marking in the row numbered the same as the question you are answering.

**6) Read the questions**

Be sure you know what the question asks! Many capable people are unsuccessful because they failed to *read* the questions correctly.

**7) Answer all questions**

Unless you have been instructed that a penalty will be deducted for incorrect answers, it is better to guess than to omit a question.

**8) Speed tests**

It is often better NOT to guess on speed tests. It has been found that on timed tests people are tempted to spend the last few seconds before time is called in marking answers at random – without even reading them – in the hope of picking up a few extra points. To discourage this practice, the instructions may warn you that your score will be "corrected" for guessing. That is, a penalty will be applied. The incorrect answers will be deducted from the correct ones, or some other penalty formula will be used.

**9) Review your answers**

If you finish before time is called, go back to the questions you guessed or omitted to give them further thought. Review other answers if you have time.

**10) Return your test materials**

If you are ready to leave before others have finished or time is called, take ALL your materials to the monitor and leave quietly. Never take any test material with you. The monitor can discover whose papers are not complete, and taking a test booklet may be grounds for disqualification.

## VIII. EXAMINATION TECHNIQUES

1) Read the general instructions carefully. These are usually printed on the first page of the exam booklet. As a rule, these instructions refer to the timing of the examination; the fact that you should not start work until the signal and must stop work at a signal, etc. If there are any *special* instructions, such as a choice of questions to be answered, make sure that you note this instruction carefully.

2) When you are ready to start work on the examination, that is as soon as the signal has been given, read the instructions to each question booklet, underline any key words or phrases, such as *least, best, outline, describe* and the like. In this way you will tend to answer as requested rather than discover on reviewing your paper that you *listed without describing*, that you selected the *worst* choice rather than the *best* choice, etc.

3) If the examination is of the objective or multiple-choice type – that is, each question will also give a series of possible answers: A, B, C or D, and you are called upon to select the best answer and write the letter next to that answer on your answer paper – it is advisable to start answering each question in turn. There may be anywhere from 50 to 100 such questions in the three or four hours allotted and you can see how much time would be taken if you read through all the questions before beginning to answer any. Furthermore, if you come across a question or group of questions which you know would be difficult to answer, it would undoubtedly affect your handling of all the other questions.

4) If the examination is of the essay type and contains but a few questions, it is a moot point as to whether you should read all the questions before starting to answer any one. Of course, if you are given a choice – say five out of seven and the like – then it is essential to read all the questions so you can eliminate the two that are most difficult. If, however, you are asked to answer all the questions, there may be danger in trying to answer the easiest one first because you may find that you will spend too much time on it. The best technique is to answer the first question, then proceed to the second, etc.

5) Time your answers. Before the exam begins, write down the time it started, then add the time allowed for the examination and write down the time it must be completed, then divide the time available somewhat as follows:
    - If 3-1/2 hours are allowed, that would be 210 minutes. If you have 80 objective-type questions, that would be an average of 2-1/2 minutes per question. Allow yourself no more than 2 minutes per question, or a total of 160 minutes, which will permit about 50 minutes to review.
    - If for the time allotment of 210 minutes there are 7 essay questions to answer, that would average about 30 minutes a question. Give yourself only 25 minutes per question so that you have about 35 minutes to review.

6) The most important instruction is to *read each question* and make sure you know what is wanted. The second most important instruction is to *time yourself properly* so that you answer every question. The third most important instruction is to *answer every question*. Guess if you have to but include something for each question. Remember that you will receive no credit for a blank and will probably receive some credit if you write something in answer to an essay question. If you guess a letter – say "B" for a multiple-choice question – you may have guessed right. If you leave a blank as an answer to a multiple choice question, the examiners may respect your feelings but it will not add a point to your score. Some exams may penalize you for wrong answers, so in such cases *only*, you may not want to guess unless you have some basis for your answer.

7) Suggestions
    a. Objective-type questions
        1. Examine the question booklet for proper sequence of pages and questions
        2. Read all instructions carefully
        3. Skip any question which seems too difficult; return to it after all other questions have been answered
        4. Apportion your time properly; do not spend too much time on any single question or group of questions

5. Note and underline key words – *all, most, fewest, least, best, worst, same, opposite,* etc.
6. Pay particular attention to negatives
7. Note unusual option, e.g., unduly long, short, complex, different or similar in content to the body of the question
8. Observe the use of "hedging" words – *probably, may, most likely,* etc.
9. Make sure that your answer is put next to the same number as the question
10. Do not second-guess unless you have good reason to believe the second answer is definitely more correct
11. Cross out original answer if you decide another answer is more accurate; do not erase until you are ready to hand your paper in
12. Answer all questions; guess unless instructed otherwise
13. Leave time for review

b. Essay questions
 1. Read each question carefully
 2. Determine exactly what is wanted. Underline key words or phrases.
 3. Decide on outline or paragraph answer
 4. Include many different points and elements unless asked to develop any one or two points or elements
 5. Show impartiality by giving pros and cons unless directed to select one side only
 6. Make and write down any assumptions you find necessary to answer the questions
 7. Watch your English, grammar, punctuation and choice of words
 8. Time your answers; don't crowd material

8) Answering the essay question

Most essay questions can be answered by framing the specific response around several key words or ideas. Here are a few such key words or ideas:

M's: manpower, materials, methods, money, management
P's: purpose, program, policy, plan, procedure, practice, problems, pitfalls, personnel, public relations
 a. Six basic steps in handling problems:
  1. Preliminary plan and background development
  2. Collect information, data and facts
  3. Analyze and interpret information, data and facts
  4. Analyze and develop solutions as well as make recommendations
  5. Prepare report and sell recommendations
  6. Install recommendations and follow up effectiveness

 b. Pitfalls to avoid
  1. *Taking things for granted* – A statement of the situation does not necessarily imply that each of the elements is necessarily true; for example, a complaint may be invalid and biased so that all that can be taken for granted is that a complaint has been registered

2. *Considering only one side of a situation* – Wherever possible, indicate several alternatives and then point out the reasons you selected the best one
3. *Failing to indicate follow up* – Whenever your answer indicates action on your part, make certain that you will take proper follow-up action to see how successful your recommendations, procedures or actions turn out to be
4. *Taking too long in answering any single question* – Remember to time your answers properly

## IX. AFTER THE TEST

Scoring procedures differ in detail among civil service jurisdictions although the general principles are the same. Whether the papers are hand-scored or graded by machine we have described, they are nearly always graded by number. That is, the person who marks the paper knows only the number – never the name – of the applicant. Not until all the papers have been graded will they be matched with names. If other tests, such as training and experience or oral interview ratings have been given, scores will be combined. Different parts of the examination usually have different weights. For example, the written test might count 60 percent of the final grade, and a rating of training and experience 40 percent. In many jurisdictions, veterans will have a certain number of points added to their grades.

After the final grade has been determined, the names are placed in grade order and an eligible list is established. There are various methods for resolving ties between those who get the same final grade – probably the most common is to place first the name of the person whose application was received first. Job offers are made from the eligible list in the order the names appear on it. You will be notified of your grade and your rank as soon as all these computations have been made. This will be done as rapidly as possible.

People who are found to meet the requirements in the announcement are called "eligibles." Their names are put on a list of eligible candidates. An eligible's chances of getting a job depend on how high he stands on this list and how fast agencies are filling jobs from the list.

When a job is to be filled from a list of eligibles, the agency asks for the names of people on the list of eligibles for that job. When the civil service commission receives this request, it sends to the agency the names of the three people highest on this list. Or, if the job to be filled has specialized requirements, the office sends the agency the names of the top three persons who meet these requirements from the general list.

The appointing officer makes a choice from among the three people whose names were sent to him. If the selected person accepts the appointment, the names of the others are put back on the list to be considered for future openings.

That is the rule in hiring from all kinds of eligible lists, whether they are for typist, carpenter, chemist, or something else. For every vacancy, the appointing officer has his choice of any one of the top three eligibles on the list. This explains why the person whose name is on top of the list sometimes does not get an appointment when some of the persons lower on the list do. If the appointing officer chooses the second or third eligible, the No. 1 eligible does not get a job at once, but stays on the list until he is appointed or the list is terminated.

# X. HOW TO PASS THE INTERVIEW TEST

The examination for which you applied requires an oral interview test. You have already taken the written test and you are now being called for the interview test – the final part of the formal examination.

You may think that it is not possible to prepare for an interview test and that there are no procedures to follow during an interview. Our purpose is to point out some things you can do in advance that will help you and some good rules to follow and pitfalls to avoid while you are being interviewed.

*What is an interview supposed to test?*

The written examination is designed to test the technical knowledge and competence of the candidate; the oral is designed to evaluate intangible qualities, not readily measured otherwise, and to establish a list showing the relative fitness of each candidate – as measured against his competitors – for the position sought. Scoring is not on the basis of "right" and "wrong," but on a sliding scale of values ranging from "not passable" to "outstanding." As a matter of fact, it is possible to achieve a relatively low score without a single "incorrect" answer because of evident weakness in the qualities being measured.

Occasionally, an examination may consist entirely of an oral test – either an individual or a group oral. In such cases, information is sought concerning the technical knowledges and abilities of the candidate, since there has been no written examination for this purpose. More commonly, however, an oral test is used to supplement a written examination.

*Who conducts interviews?*

The composition of oral boards varies among different jurisdictions. In nearly all, a representative of the personnel department serves as chairman. One of the members of the board may be a representative of the department in which the candidate would work. In some cases, "outside experts" are used, and, frequently, a businessman or some other representative of the general public is asked to serve. Labor and management or other special groups may be represented. The aim is to secure the services of experts in the appropriate field.

However the board is composed, it is a good idea (and not at all improper or unethical) to ascertain in advance of the interview who the members are and what groups they represent. When you are introduced to them, you will have some idea of their backgrounds and interests, and at least you will not stutter and stammer over their names.

*What should be done before the interview?*

While knowledge about the board members is useful and takes some of the surprise element out of the interview, there is other preparation which is more substantive. It *is* possible to prepare for an oral interview – in several ways:

**1) Keep a copy of your application and review it carefully before the interview**

This may be the only document before the oral board, and the starting point of the interview. Know what education and experience you have listed there, and the sequence and dates of all of it. Sometimes the board will ask you to review the highlights of your experience for them; you should not have to hem and haw doing it.

**2) Study the class specification and the examination announcement**

Usually, the oral board has one or both of these to guide them. The qualities, characteristics or knowledges required by the position sought are stated in these documents. They offer valuable clues as to the nature of the oral interview. For example, if the job involves supervisory responsibilities, the announcement will usually indicate that knowledge of modern supervisory methods and the qualifications of the candidate as a supervisor will be tested. If so, you can expect such questions, frequently in the form of a hypothetical situation which you are expected to solve. NEVER go into an oral without knowledge of the duties and responsibilities of the job you seek.

### 3) Think through each qualification required

Try to visualize the kind of questions you would ask if you were a board member. How well could you answer them? Try especially to appraise your own knowledge and background in each area, *measured against the job sought*, and identify any areas in which you are weak. Be critical and realistic – do not flatter yourself.

### 4) Do some general reading in areas in which you feel you may be weak

For example, if the job involves supervision and your past experience has NOT, some general reading in supervisory methods and practices, particularly in the field of human relations, might be useful. Do NOT study agency procedures or detailed manuals. The oral board will be testing your understanding and capacity, not your memory.

### 5) Get a good night's sleep and watch your general health and mental attitude

You will want a clear head at the interview. Take care of a cold or any other minor ailment, and of course, no hangovers.

*What should be done on the day of the interview?*

Now comes the day of the interview itself. Give yourself plenty of time to get there. Plan to arrive somewhat ahead of the scheduled time, particularly if your appointment is in the fore part of the day. If a previous candidate fails to appear, the board might be ready for you a bit early. By early afternoon an oral board is almost invariably behind schedule if there are many candidates, and you may have to wait. Take along a book or magazine to read, or your application to review, but leave any extraneous material in the waiting room when you go in for your interview. In any event, relax and compose yourself.

The matter of dress is important. The board is forming impressions about you – from your experience, your manners, your attitude, and your appearance. Give your personal appearance careful attention. Dress your best, but not your flashiest. Choose conservative, appropriate clothing, and be sure it is immaculate. This is a business interview, and your appearance should indicate that you regard it as such. Besides, being well groomed and properly dressed will help boost your confidence.

Sooner or later, someone will call your name and escort you into the interview room. *This is it.* From here on you are on your own. It is too late for any more preparation. But remember, you asked for this opportunity to prove your fitness, and you are here because your request was granted.

*What happens when you go in?*

The usual sequence of events will be as follows: The clerk (who is often the board stenographer) will introduce you to the chairman of the oral board, who will introduce you to the other members of the board. Acknowledge the introductions before you sit down. Do not be surprised if you find a microphone facing you or a stenotypist sitting by. Oral interviews are usually recorded in the event of an appeal or other review.

Usually the chairman of the board will open the interview by reviewing the highlights of your education and work experience from your application – primarily for the benefit of the other members of the board, as well as to get the material into the record. Do not interrupt or comment unless there is an error or significant misinterpretation; if that is the case, do not hesitate. But do not quibble about insignificant matters. Also, he will usually ask you some question about your education, experience or your present job – partly to get you to start talking and to establish the interviewing "rapport." He may start the actual questioning, or turn it over to one of the other members. Frequently, each member undertakes the questioning on a particular area, one in which he is perhaps most competent, so you can expect each member to participate in the examination. Because time is limited, you may also expect some rather abrupt switches in the direction the questioning takes, so do not be upset by it. Normally, a board member will not pursue a single line of questioning unless he discovers a particular strength or weakness.

After each member has participated, the chairman will usually ask whether any member has any further questions, then will ask you if you have anything you wish to add. Unless you are expecting this question, it may floor you. Worse, it may start you off on an extended, extemporaneous speech. The board is not usually seeking more information. The question is principally to offer you a last opportunity to present further qualifications or to indicate that you have nothing to add. So, if you feel that a significant qualification or characteristic has been overlooked, it is proper to point it out in a sentence or so. Do not compliment the board on the thoroughness of their examination – they have been sketchy, and you know it. If you wish, merely say, "No thank you, I have nothing further to add." This is a point where you can "talk yourself out" of a good impression or fail to present an important bit of information. Remember, *you close the interview yourself*.

The chairman will then say, "That is all, Mr. _____, thank you." Do not be startled; the interview is over, and quicker than you think. Thank him, gather your belongings and take your leave. Save your sigh of relief for the other side of the door.

*How to put your best foot forward*

Throughout this entire process, you may feel that the board individually and collectively is trying to pierce your defenses, seek out your hidden weaknesses and embarrass and confuse you. Actually, this is not true. They are obliged to make an appraisal of your qualifications for the job you are seeking, and they want to see you in your best light. Remember, they must interview all candidates and a non-cooperative candidate may become a failure in spite of their best efforts to bring out his qualifications. Here are 15 suggestions that will help you:

**1) Be natural – Keep your attitude confident, not cocky**

If you are not confident that you can do the job, do not expect the board to be. Do not apologize for your weaknesses, try to bring out your strong points. The board is interested in a positive, not negative, presentation. Cockiness will antagonize any board member and make him wonder if you are covering up a weakness by a false show of strength.

**2) Get comfortable, but don't lounge or sprawl**

Sit erectly but not stiffly. A careless posture may lead the board to conclude that you are careless in other things, or at least that you are not impressed by the importance of the occasion. Either conclusion is natural, even if incorrect. Do not fuss with your clothing, a pencil or an ashtray. Your hands may occasionally be useful to emphasize a point; do not let them become a point of distraction.

**3) Do not wisecrack or make small talk**

This is a serious situation, and your attitude should show that you consider it as such. Further, the time of the board is limited – they do not want to waste it, and neither should you.

**4) Do not exaggerate your experience or abilities**

In the first place, from information in the application or other interviews and sources, the board may know more about you than you think. Secondly, you probably will not get away with it. An experienced board is rather adept at spotting such a situation, so do not take the chance.

**5) If you know a board member, do not make a point of it, yet do not hide it**

Certainly you are not fooling him, and probably not the other members of the board. Do not try to take advantage of your acquaintanceship – it will probably do you little good.

**6) Do not dominate the interview**

Let the board do that. They will give you the clues – do not assume that you have to do all the talking. Realize that the board has a number of questions to ask you, and do not try to take up all the interview time by showing off your extensive knowledge of the answer to the first one.

**7) Be attentive**

You only have 20 minutes or so, and you should keep your attention at its sharpest throughout. When a member is addressing a problem or question to you, give him your undivided attention. Address your reply principally to him, but do not exclude the other board members.

**8) Do not interrupt**

A board member may be stating a problem for you to analyze. He will ask you a question when the time comes. Let him state the problem, and wait for the question.

**9) Make sure you understand the question**

Do not try to answer until you are sure what the question is. If it is not clear, restate it in your own words or ask the board member to clarify it for you. However, do not haggle about minor elements.

**10) Reply promptly but not hastily**

A common entry on oral board rating sheets is "candidate responded readily," or "candidate hesitated in replies." Respond as promptly and quickly as you can, but do not jump to a hasty, ill-considered answer.

**11) Do not be peremptory in your answers**

A brief answer is proper – but do not fire your answer back. That is a losing game from your point of view. The board member can probably ask questions much faster than you can answer them.

**12) Do not try to create the answer you think the board member wants**

He is interested in what kind of mind you have and how it works – not in playing games. Furthermore, he can usually spot this practice and will actually grade you down on it.

**13) Do not switch sides in your reply merely to agree with a board member**

Frequently, a member will take a contrary position merely to draw you out and to see if you are willing and able to defend your point of view. Do not start a debate, yet do not surrender a good position. If a position is worth taking, it is worth defending.

**14) Do not be afraid to admit an error in judgment if you are shown to be wrong**

The board knows that you are forced to reply without any opportunity for careful consideration. Your answer may be demonstrably wrong. If so, admit it and get on with the interview.

**15) Do not dwell at length on your present job**

The opening question may relate to your present assignment. Answer the question but do not go into an extended discussion. You are being examined for a *new* job, not your present one. As a matter of fact, try to phrase ALL your answers in terms of the job for which you are being examined.

*Basis of Rating*

Probably you will forget most of these "do's" and "don'ts" when you walk into the oral interview room. Even remembering them all will not ensure you a passing grade. Perhaps you did not have the qualifications in the first place. But remembering them will help you to put your best foot forward, without treading on the toes of the board members.

Rumor and popular opinion to the contrary notwithstanding, an oral board wants you to make the best appearance possible. They know you are under pressure – but they also want to see how you respond to it as a guide to what your reaction would be under the pressures of the job you seek. They will be influenced by the degree of poise you display, the personal traits you show and the manner in which you respond.


ABOUT THIS BOOK

This book contains tests divided into Examination Sections. Go through each test, answering every question in the margin. We have also attached a sample answer sheet at the back of the book that can be removed and used. At the end of each test look at the answer key and check your answers. On the ones you got wrong, look at the right answer choice and learn. Do not fill in the answers first. Do not memorize the questions and answers, but understand the answer and principles involved. On your test, the questions will likely be different from the samples. Questions are changed and new ones added. If you understand these past questions you should have success with any changes that arise. Tests may consist of several types of questions. We have additional books on each subject should more study be advisable or necessary for you. Finally, the more you study, the better prepared you will be. This book is intended to be the last thing you study before you walk into the examination room. Prior study of relevant texts is also recommended. NLC publishes some of these in our Fundamental Series. Knowledge and good sense are important factors in passing your exam. Good luck also helps. So now study this Passbook, absorb the material contained within and take that knowledge into the examination. Then do your best to pass that exam.

# EXAMINATION SECTION

# EXAMINATION SECTION
# TEST 1

DIRECTIONS: Each question or incomplete statement is followed by several suggested answers or completions. Select the one that BEST answers the question or completes the statement. *PRINT THE LETTER OF THE CORRECT ANSWER IN THE SPACE AT THE RIGHT.*

Questions 1-17.

DIRECTIONS: Questions 1 through 17 are to be answered on the basis of the tools shown below and on the following page. The numbers in the answers refer to the numbers beneath the tools.

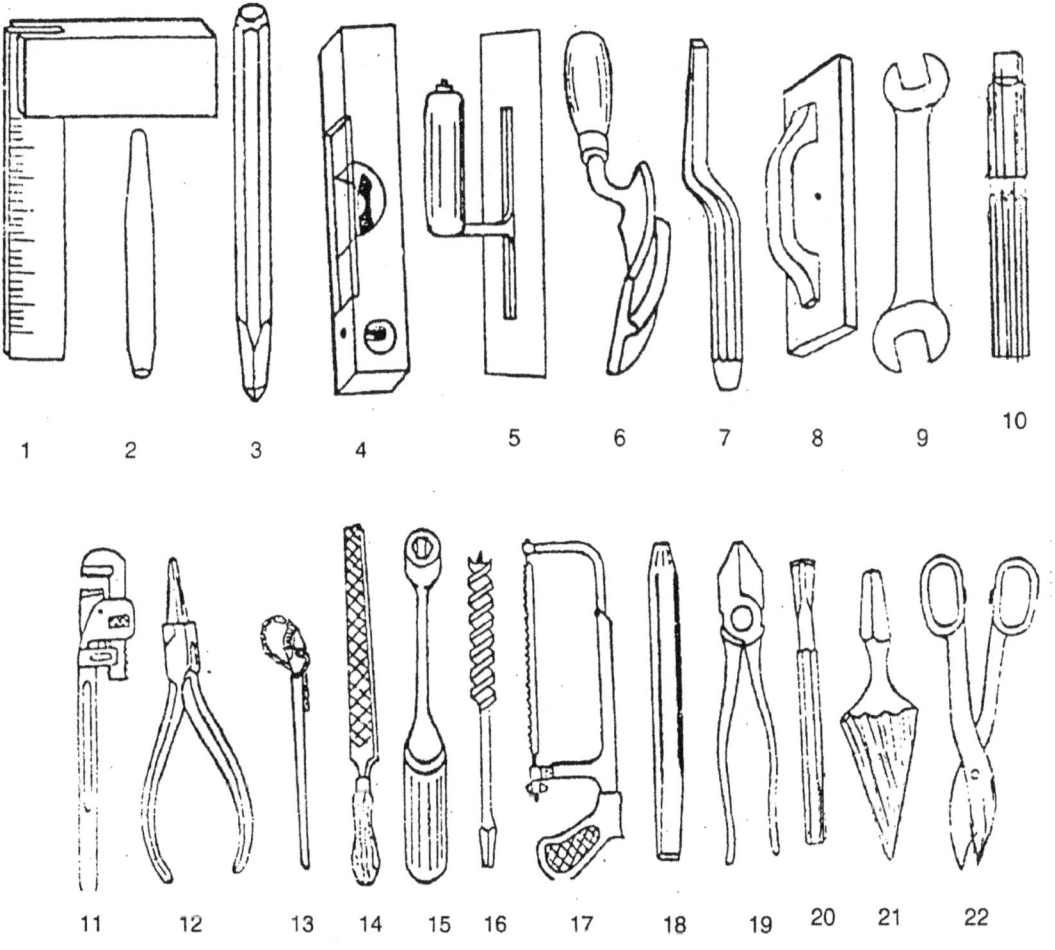

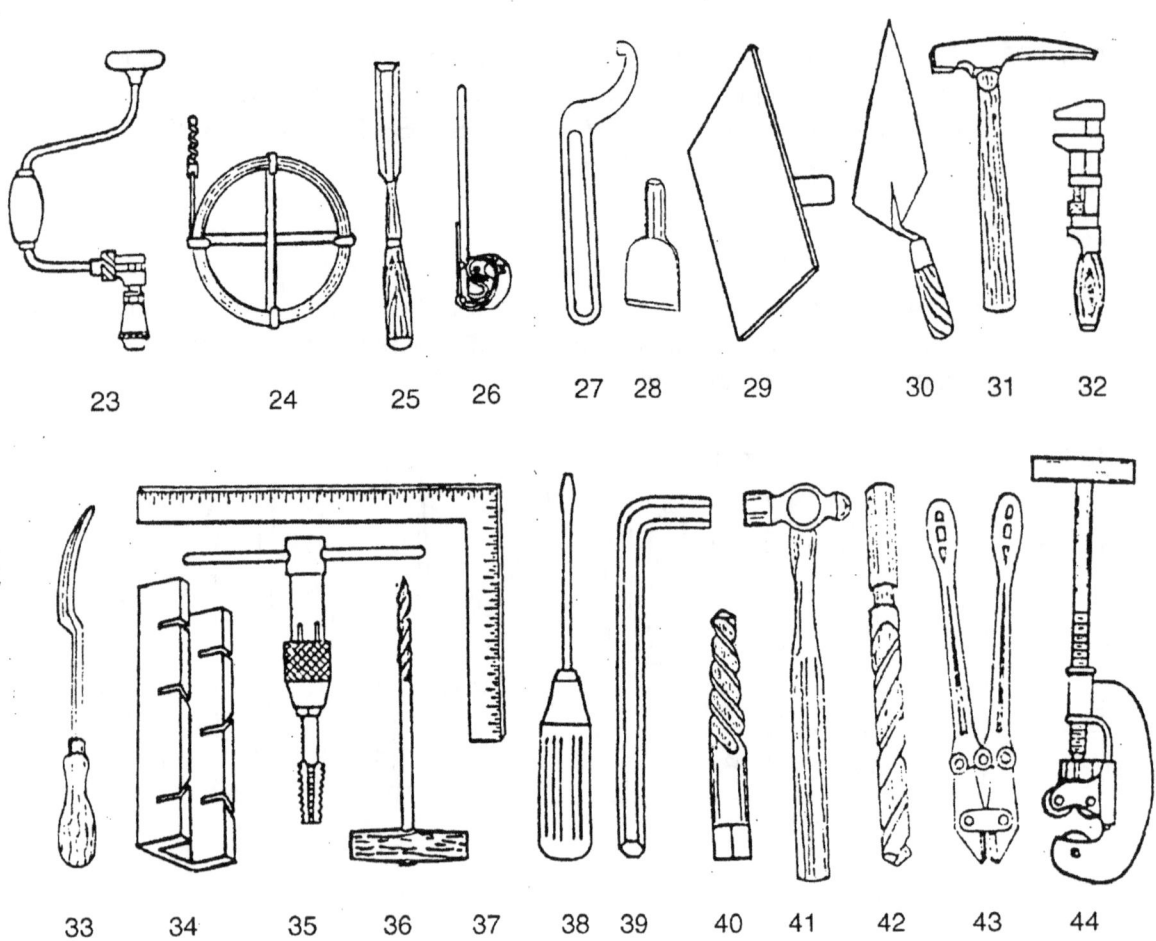

1. To tighten an elbow onto a threaded pipe, a mechanic should use tool number
   A. 9   B. 11   C. 26   D. 32

2. To cut grooves in newly poured cement, a mechanic should use tool number
   A. 5   B. 6   C. 28   D. 29

3. To *caulk* a lead joint, a mechanic should use tool number
   A. 7   B. 10   C. 25   D. 33

4. The term *snips* should be applied by a mechanic to tool number
   A. 12   B. 22   C. 36   D. 43

5. To slightly enlarge an existing 17/32" diameter hole in a metal plate, a mechanic should use tool number
   A. 3   B. 10   C. 14   D. 35

6. The term *snake* should be applied by a mechanic to tool number
   A. 21   B. 23   C. 24   D. 40

7. If the threaded portion of a 1/2" brass pipe breaks off inside a gate valve, the piece should be removed with tool number

   A. 15   B. 35   C. 39   D. 40

8. To cut a face brick into a bat, a mechanic should use tool number

   A. 3   B. 18   C. 25   D. 28

9. A mechanic should cut a 3" x 2" x 3/16" angle iron with tool number

   A. 3   B. 17   C. 22   D. 43

10. A mechanic should tighten a chrome-plated water supply pipe by using tool number

    A. 11   B. 19   C. 26   D. 32

11. The term *hawk* should be applied by a mechanic to tool number

    A. 28   B. 29   C. 30   D. 33

12. If your co-worker asks you to pass him the *star* drill, you should hand him tool number

    A. 16   B. 20   C. 40   D. 42

13. After threading a 1" diameter piece of pipe, a mechanic should debur the inside by using tool number

    A. 14   B. 21   C. 36   D. 40

14. A mechanic should apply the term *float* to tool number

    A. 4   B. 6   C. 8   D. 28

15. If a mechanic has to cut a dozen 15-inch lengths of 3/4-inch steel pipe for spacers, he should use tool number

    A. 18   B. 26   C. 43   D. 44

16. If a mechanic is erecting two structural steel plates and needs to line up the bolt holes, he should use tool number

    A. 2   B. 3   C. 33   D. 42

17. To cut reinforcing wire mesh to be used in a concrete floor, you should use tool number

    A. 7   B. 17   C. 18   D. 43

18. The MAIN reason for overhauling a power tool on a regular basis is to

    A. make the men more familiar with the tool
    B. keep the men busy during slack times
    C. insure that the tool is used occasionally
    D. minimize breakdowns

19. A mechanic should NOT press too heavily on a hacksaw while using it to cut through a steel rod because this may

    A. create flying steel particles    B. bend the frame
    C. break the blade                  D. overheat the rod

20. Creosote is commonly used with wood to

   A. speed-up the seasoning
   B. make the wood fireproof
   C. make painting easier
   D. preserve the wood

21. A mitre box should be used to

   A. hold a saw while sharpening it
   B. store expensive tools
   C. hold a saw at a fixed angle
   D. encase steel beams for protection

22. Wood scaffold planks should be inspected

   A. at regular intervals
   B. before they are stored away
   C. once a week
   D. each time before they are used

23. Continuous sheeting should be used when excavating deep trenches in

   A. rock
   B. stiff clay
   C. firm earth
   D. unstable soil

24. The MAIN reason for requiring that certain special tools be returned to the tool room after a job has been completed is that

   A. missing tools can be replaced
   B. the men will not need to care for the tools
   C. more tools will be available for use
   D. this permits easier inspection and maintenance of tools

25. The BEST material to use to extinguish an oil fire is

   A. sand
   B. water
   C. sawdust
   D. stone gravel

26. A *lally* column is

   A. fabricated from angles and plates
   B. fabricated by tying two channels together with lattice bars
   C. a steel member that has unequal sections
   D. a pipe fitted with a base plate at each end

27. The BEST action for you to take if you discover a small puddle of oil on the shop floor is to FIRST

   A. have it cleaned up
   B. find out who spilled it
   C. discover the source of the leak
   D. cover it with newspaper

28. You should listen to your foreman even when he insists on explaining the procedure for a job you have done many times before because

   A. you can do the job the way you want when he leaves
   B. he may make an error and you can show that you know your job
   C. it is wise to humor him even if he is wrong
   D. you are required to do the job the way the foreman wants it

Questions 29-34.

DIRECTIONS: Questions 29 through 34 refer to the sketches shown to the right of each question.

29. The indicated pressure is MOST NEARLY _____ psi.
   A. 132
   B. 137
   C. 143
   D. 148

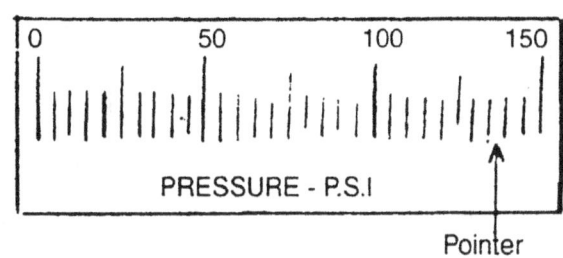

30. The fewest number of shims, of any combination of thicknesses, required to exactly fill the 1/4" gap shown is
   A. 7
   B. 8
   C. 9
   D. 10

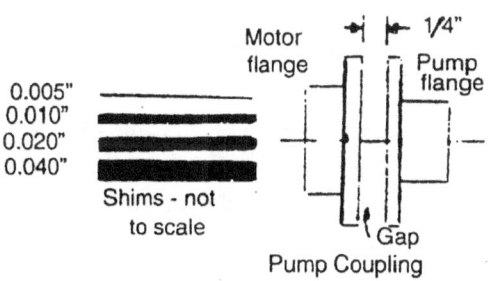

31. The dimension X on the keyway shown is
   A. 3 3/8"
   B. 3 9/16"
   C. 3 3/4"
   D. 4"

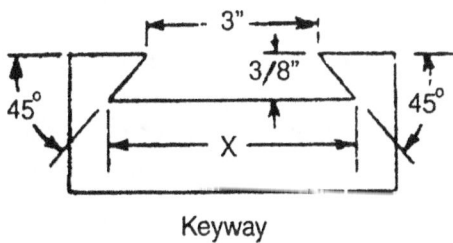

32. If the tank gage reads 120 psi, then the pipe gage should read _____ psi.
   A. 80
   B. 120
   C. 180
   D. 240

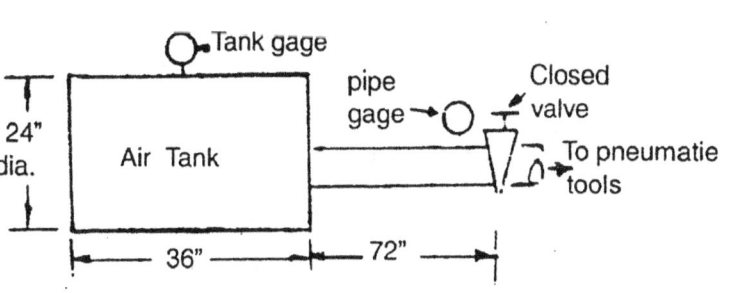

33. The MINIMUM number of feet of chainlink fence needed to completely enclose the storage yard shown is
    A. 278
    B. 286
    C. 295
    D. 304

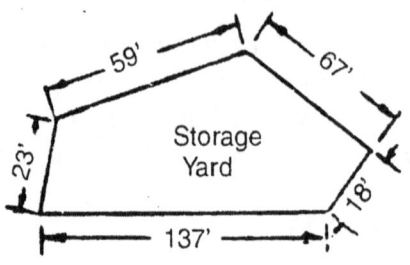

34. The distance $X$ between the holes is
    A. 1 7/8"
    B. 2 1/16"
    C. 2 3/8"
    D. 2 9/16"

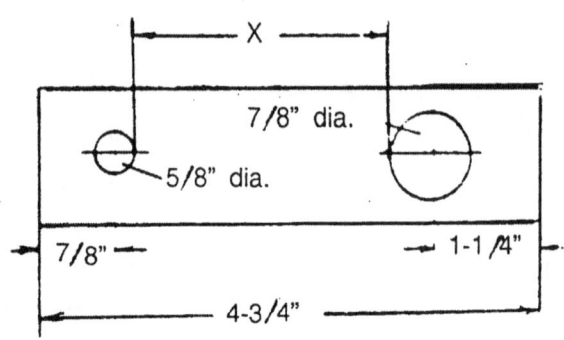

35. A rule of the Transit Authority is that all employees are required to report defective equipment to their superiors, even when the maintenance of the particular equipment is handled by someone else.
    The MAIN purpose of this rule is to
    A. determine who is doing his job improperly
    B. have repairs made before trouble occurs
    C. encourage all employees to be alert at all times
    D. reduce the cost of equipment

36. Some equipment is fitted with wing nuts.
    Such nuts are especially useful when
    A. the nut is to be wired closed
    B. space is limited
    C. the equipment is subject to vibration
    D. the nuts must be removed frequently

37. It is considered bad practice to use water to put out electrical fires MAINLY because the water may
    A. rust the equipment
    B. short circuit the lines
    C. cause a serious shock
    D. damage the electrical insulation

38. While you are being trained, you will be assigned to work with an experienced mechanic.
    It would be BEST for you to
    A. remind the mechanic that he is responsible for your training
    B. tell him frequently how much you know about the work
    C. let him do all the work while you observe closely
    D. be as cooperative and helpful as you can

39. The BEST instrument to use to make certain that two points, separated by a vertical distance of 9 feet, are in perfect vertical alignment is a

    A. square  B. level  C. plumb bob  D. protractor

40. If a measurement scaled from a drawing is one inch, and the scale of the drawing is 1/8-inch to the foot, then the one inch measurement would represent an actual length of

    A. 8 feet
    B. 2 feet
    C. 1/8 of a foot
    D. 8 inches

---

## KEY (CORRECT ANSWERS)

| | | | | | | | |
|---|---|---|---|---|---|---|---|
| 1. | B | 11. | B | 21. | C | 31. | C |
| 2. | B | 12. | B | 22. | D | 32. | B |
| 3. | A | 13. | B | 23. | D | 33. | D |
| 4. | B | 14. | C | 24. | D | 34. | A |
| 5. | B | 15. | D | 25. | A | 35. | B |
| 6. | C | 16. | A | 26. | D | 36. | D |
| 7. | D | 17. | D | 27. | A | 37. | C |
| 8. | D | 18. | D | 28. | D | 38. | D |
| 9. | B | 19. | C | 29. | B | 39. | C |
| 10. | C | 20. | D | 30. | A | 40. | A |

# TEST 2

DIRECTIONS: Each question or incomplete statement is followed by several suggested answers or completions. Select the one that BEST answers the question or completes the statement. *PRINT THE LETTER OF THE CORRECT ANSWER IN THE SPACE AT THE RIGHT.*

1. Cloth tapes should NOT be used when accurate measurements must be obtained because  1.____

    A. the numbers soon become worn and thus difficult to read
    B. there are not enough subdivisions of each inch on the tape
    C. the ink runs when wet, thus making the tape difficult to read
    D. small changes in the pull on the tape will make considerable differences in tape readings

2. It is considered good practice to release the pressure from an air hose before uncoupling the hose connection because this avoids  2.____

    A. wasting air
    B. possible personal injury
    C. damage to the air tool
    D. damage to the air compressor

3. In brick construction, a structural steel member is used to support the wall above door and window openings. This member is called a  3.____

    A. purlin        B. sill        C. truss        D. lintel

Questions 4-9.

DIRECTIONS: Questions 4 through 9 show the top view of an object in the first column, the front view of the same object in the second column and four drawings in the third column, one of which correctly represents the RIGHT side view of the object. Select the CORRECT right side view. As a guide, the first one is an illustrative example, the CORRECT answer of which is C.

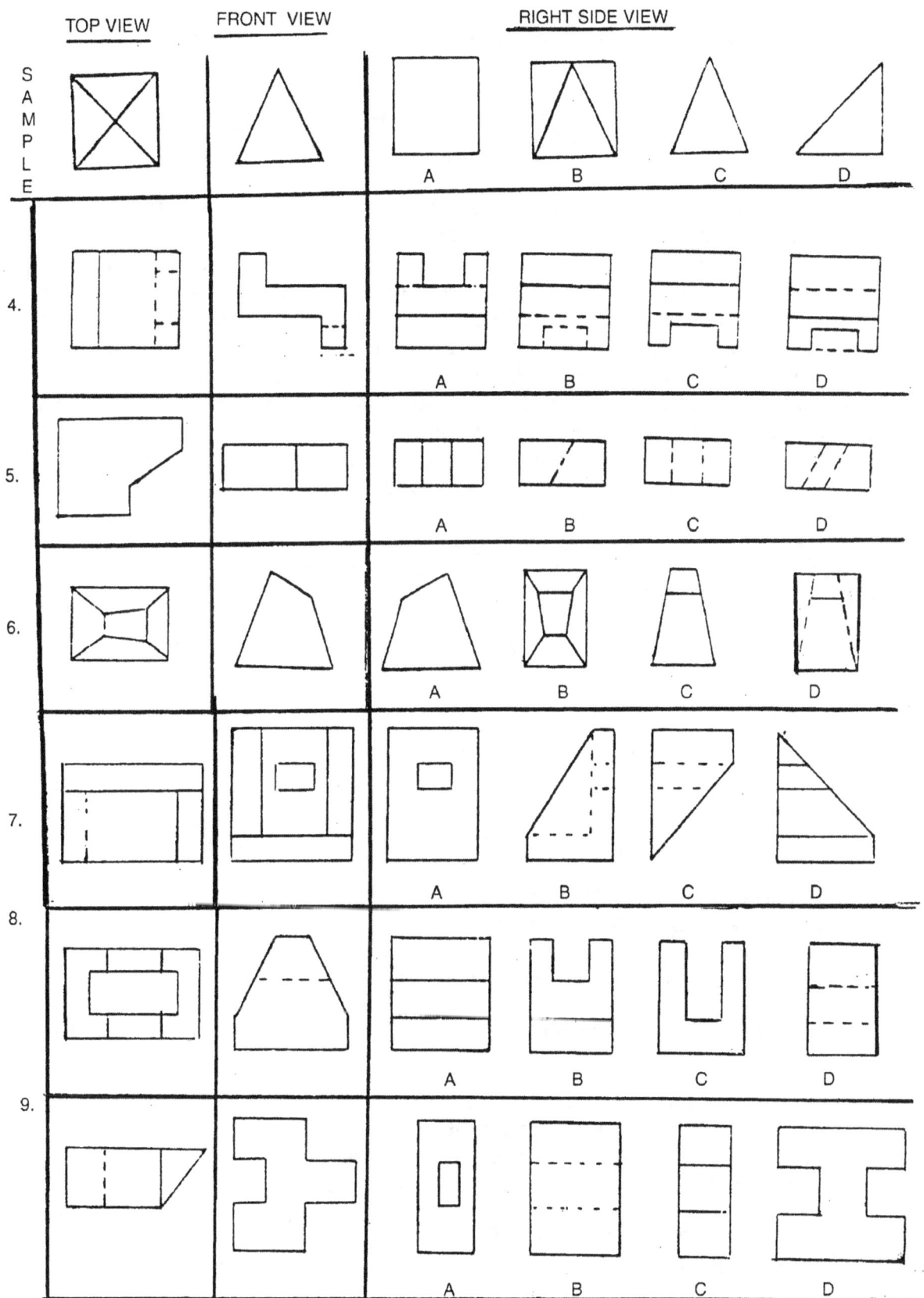

Questions 10-14.

DIRECTIONS: Questions 10 through 14 are to be answered on the basis of the information contained in the safety regulations given below. In answering these questions, refer to these rules.

## REGULATIONS FOR SMALL GROUPS WHO MOVE FROM POINT TO POINT ON THE TRACKS

*Employees who perform duties on the tracks in small groups and who move from point to point along the trainway must be on the alert at all times and prepared to clear the track when a train approaches without unnecessarily slowing it down. Underground at all times, and out-of-doors between sunset and sunrise, such employees must not enter upon the tracks unless each of them is equipped with an approved light. Flashlights must not be used for protection by such groups. Upon clearing the track to permit a train to pass, each member of the group must give a proceed signal, by hand or light, to the motorman of the train. Whenever such small groups are working in an area protected by caution lights or flags, but are not members of the gang for whom the flagging protection was established, they must not give proceed signals to motormen. The purpose of this rule is to avoid a motorman's confusing such signal with that of the flagman who is protecting a gang. Whenever a small group is engaged in work of an engrossing nature or at any time when the view of approaching trains is limited by reason of curves or otherwise, one man of the group, equipped with a whistle, must be assigned properly to warn and protect the man or men at work and must not perform any other duties while so assigned.*

10. If a small group of men are traveling along the tracks toward their work location and a train approaches, they should

    A. stop the train
    B. signal the motorman to go slowly
    C. clear the track
    D. stop immediately

11. Small groups may enter upon the tracks

    A. only between sunset and sunrise
    B. provided each has an approved light
    C. provided their foreman has a good flashlight
    D. provided each man has an approved flashlight

12. After a small group has cleared the tracks in an area unprotected by caution lights or flags,

    A. each member must give the proceed signal to the motorman
    B. the foreman signals the motorman to proceed
    C. the motorman can proceed provided he goes slowly
    D. the last member off the tracks gives the signal to the motorman

13. If a small group is working in an area protected by the signals of a track gang, the members of the small group

    A. need not be concerned with train movement
    B. must give the proceed signal together with the track gang

C. can delegate one of their members to give the proceed signal
D. must not give the proceed signal

14. If the view of approaching trains is blocked, the small group should

A. move to where they can see the trains
B. delegate one of the group to warn and protect them
C. keep their ears alert for approaching trains
D. refuse to work at such locations

14.____

15. The information in an accident report which may be MOST useful in helping to prevent similar-type accidents from happening is the

A. cause of the accident
B. time of day it happened
C. type of injuries suffered
D. number of people injured

15.____

16. The MAIN reason why each coat of paint should be of a different color when two coats of paint are specified is that

A. cheaper paint can be used as the undercoat
B. less care need be taken in applying the coats
C. any missed areas will be easier to spot
D. the colors do not have to be exact

16.____

Questions 17-23.

DIRECTIONS: Questions 17 through 23 refer to the sketches shown to the right of each question.

17. The distance y is
A. 5/8"
B. 7/8"
C. 1 1/8"
D. 1 3/8"

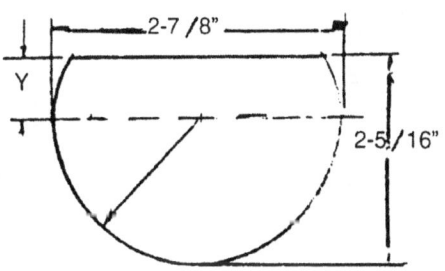

17.____

18. The sketch shows the float-operated trippers for operating a sump pump. If you want the pump to start sooner, you should _____ tripper.
A. *lower* the upper
B. *lower* the lower
C. *raise* the upper
D. *raise* the lower

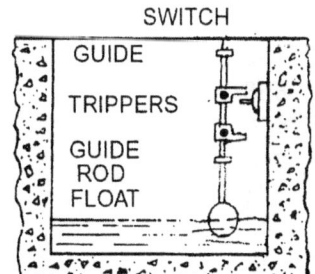

18.____

19. The width of the wood stud shown is
    A. 1 1/8"
    B. 1 5/16"
    C. 1 5/8"
    D. 3 5/8"

19.___

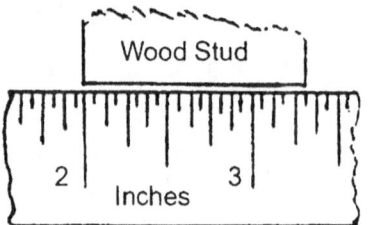

20. The right angle shown has been divided into four unequal parts.
    The number of degrees in angle X is
    A. 31°
    B. 33°
    C. 38°
    D. 45°

20.___

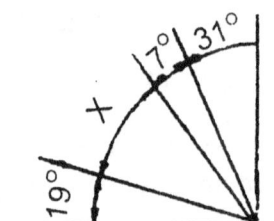

21. The reading on the meter shown is MOST NEARLY
    A. 0465
    B. 0475
    C. 0566
    D. 1566

21.___

22. The length X of the slot shown is
    A. 2 3/8"
    B. 2 7/16"
    C. 2 1/2"
    D. 2 9/16"

22.___

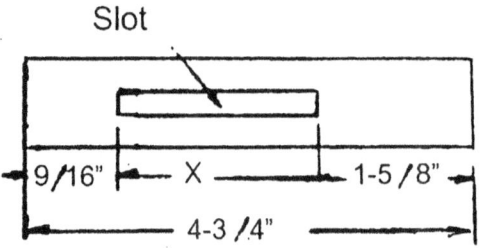

23. The volume of the bar shown is _____ cubic inches.
    A. 132
    B. 356
    C. 420
    D. 516

23.___

24. Gaskets should be used with

    A. flanged pipe fittings           B. bell and spigot pipe
    C. threaded reducing couplings     D. threaded bushings

24.___

25. The MAIN purpose for providing a plumbing fixture with a trap is to

    A. equalize the pressures in the drainage system
    B. catch any article that might plug the drain
    C. prevent passage of gases
    D. supply an easy means of cleaning if the fixture gets plugged

26. The *soil stack* of a drainage system is left open at its upper end in order to

    A. prevent the sewer from backing up into the traps
    B. prevent the siphoning of traps
    C. prevent ventilation of the drainage system
    D. hold a vacuum above the house drain line

27. Under the city color coding of pipes, drinking water pipes should be painted

    A. blue    B. yellow    C. green    D. red

28. When changing from a 2" pipe size to a 1" pipe in a horizontal steam line, the PROPER fitting to be used is a(n)

    A. concentric bushing          B. face bushing
    C. concentric reducer          D. eccentric reducer

29. An expansion slip joint

    A. permits longitudinal movement of a pipe
    B. is used when the pipe has been cut short
    C. compensates for differences in pipe pressure
    D. permits small movement for lining pipe hangers

30. The MAIN reason why brass is better than iron for water piping is that brass is

    A. cheaper                     B. lighter
    C. stronger                    D. more corrosion resistant

31. A bell and spigot cast iron pipe joint is made water-tight by

    A. rolling and beading the ends
    B. caulking with oakum and lead
    C. caulking with cotton wick and cement
    D. applying sealing compound to the threaded ends

32. The one of the following valves which is ALWAYS automatic in operation is the _____ valve.

    A. gate    B. angle    C. check    D. globe

33. Threaded joints may be made up tight by using pipe thread compound. The CORRECT procedure is to apply the compound

    A. only to the male threads
    B. only to the female threads
    C. to both male and female threads
    D. to either the male or female thread, depending on the pipe size

Questions 34-39.

DIRECTIONS: Questions 34 through 39 are to be answered on the basis of the riser diagram shown below.

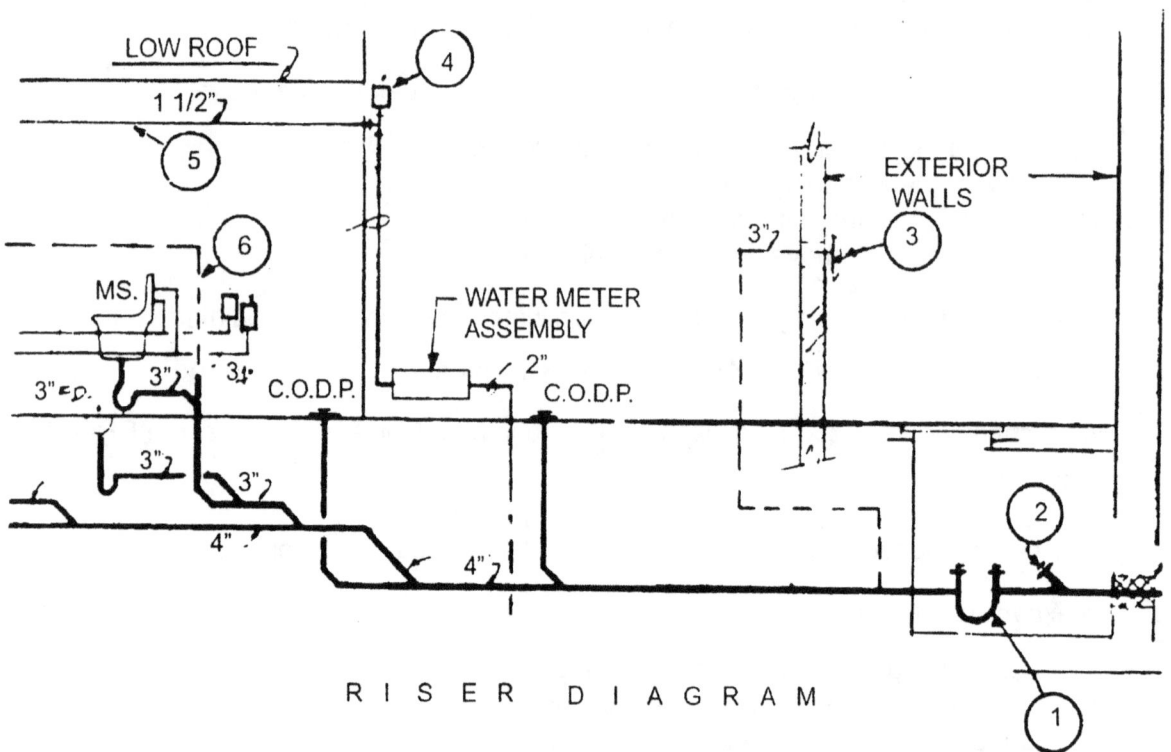

RISER DIAGRAM

34. Fitting 1 is a

    A. floor drain      B. trap
    C. clean out      D. check valve

35. Fitting 2 is a

    A. floor drain      B. trap
    C. clean out      D. check valve

36. Fitting 3 is a

    A. fire department connection
    B. sprinkler head
    C. valve
    D. fresh air inlet

37. Fitting 4 is a(n)

    A. gate valve      B. air chamber
    C. running trap      D. vent inlet

38. Line 5 is a

    A. hot water pipe
    B. vent line
    C. cold water line
    D. soil line

39. Line 6 is a _____ line.

    A. vent
    B. cold water
    C. hot water
    D. drain

40. A non-rising stem-type gate valve is especially useful when

    A. the stem must move downward only
    B. the pressure in the pipe must remain constant
    C. clearances around the valve are limited
    D. hand control of the valve is not required

# KEY (CORRECT ANSWERS)

| | | | |
|---|---|---|---|
| 1. D | 11. B | 21. A | 31. B |
| 2. B | 12. A | 22. D | 32. C |
| 3. D | 13. D | 23. C | 33. A |
| 4. C | 14. B | 24. A | 34. B |
| 5. A | 15. A | 25. C | 35. C |
| 6. C | 16. C | 26. B | 36. D |
| 7. B | 17. B | 27. C | 37. B |
| 8. B | 18. D | 28. D | 38. C |
| 9. C | 19. B | 29. A | 39. A |
| 10. C | 20. B | 30. D | 40. C |

# EXAMINATION SECTION
# TEST 1

DIRECTIONS: Each question or incomplete statement is followed by several suggested answers or completions. Select the one that BEST answers the question or completes the statement. *PRINT THE LETTER OF THE CORRECT ANSWER IN THE SPACE AT THE RIGHT.*

1. It is NOT good practice to cut thin-walled copper tubing with an ordinary three-wheel pipe cutter because

    A. the cutters will be dulled
    B. too much time is required
    C. the tubing end must be reamed after cutting
    D. the tubing is likely to collapse

    1._____

2. Wedges are used under vertical shoring timbers to

    A. utilize scrap wood
    B. permit the use of very short timbers
    C. obtain rigid shoring
    D. absorb construction noise

    2._____

3. The longest nail of the following is a _____-penny nail.

    A. 12      B. 10      C. 6      D. 4

    3._____

4. A commonly used priming coat for structural steel is

    A. enamel      B. varnish      C. red lead      D. lacquer

    4._____

5. A nail set is a tool used for

    A. straightening bent nails
    B. cutting nails to specified size
    C. sinking a nail head in wood
    D. measuring nail size

    5._____

6. The fine aggregate used in concrete is

    A. cement
    C. cinder
    B. heavy broken stone
    D. sand

    6._____

7. Wood forms designed to hold poured concrete should be

    A. water-tight
    C. dust-tight
    B. air-tight
    D. termite-proof

    7._____

8. Hollow tile block *generally* has corrugated outer surfaces in order to

    A. prevent glazing of the tile
    B. secure strong bonding
    C. prevent expansion of the tile
    D. give a decorative effect

    8._____

QUESTIONS 9-16.

Questions 9 to 16 inclusive are based on the ladder safety rules given below. Read these rules carefully before answering these items.

## LADDER SAFETY RULES

When a ladder is placed on a slightly uneven supporting surface, use a flat piece of board or small wedge to even up the ladder feet. To secure the proper angle for resting a ladder, it should be placed so that the distance from the base of the ladder to the supporting wall is 1/4 the length of the ladder. To avoid overloading a ladder, only one person should work on a ladder at a time. Do not place a ladder in front of a door. When the top rung of a ladder rests against a pole, the ladder should be lashed securely. Clear loose stones or debris from the ground around the base of a ladder before climbing. While on a ladder do not attempt to lean so that any part of the body, except arms or hands, extends more than 12 inches beyond the side rail. Always face the ladder when ascending or descending. When carrying ladders through buildings, watch for ceiling globes and lighting fixtures. Avoid the use of rolling ladders as scaffold supports.

9. A small wedge is used to

   A. even up the feet of a ladder resting on an uneven surface
   B. lock the wheels of a roller ladder
   C. secure the proper resting angle for a ladder
   D. secure a ladder against a pole

10. An 8 foot ladder resting against a wall should be so inclined that the distance between the base of the ladder and the wall is _____ feet.

    A. 2     B. 5     C. 7     D. 9

11. A ladder should be lashed securely when

    A. it is placed in front of a door
    B. loose stones are on the ground near the base of the ladder
    C. the top rung rests against a pole
    D. two people are working from the same ladder

12. Rolling ladders

    A. should be used for scaffold supports
    B. should not be used for scaffold supports
    C. are useful on uneven ground
    D. should be used against a pole

13. When carrying a ladder through a building it is necessary to

    A. have two men to carry it
    B. carry the ladder vertically
    C. watch for ceiling globes
    D. face the ladder while carrying it

14. It is POOR practice to

    A. lash a ladder securely at any time
    B. clear debris from the base of a ladder before climbing
    C. even up the feet of a ladder resting on slightly uneven ground
    D. place a ladder in front of a door

15. A person on a ladder should NOT extend his head beyond the side rail by more than _____ inches.

    A. 12      B. 9      C. 7      D. 5

16. The MOST important reason for permitting only one person to work on a ladder at a time is that

    A. both could not face the ladder at one time
    B. the ladder will be overloaded
    C. time would be lost going up and down the ladder
    D. they would obstruct each other

17. A masonry nail is shown in sketch No.
    A. 1
    B. 2
    C. 3
    D. 4

18. This sketch shows a gauge used to
    A. measure the depth of a hole
    B. determine if a board has been smoothly planed
    C. check the width of a brick
    D. scribe a line on a board parallel to its edge

19. Two bars are to be riveted together. The riveted connection which would be STRONGEST is No.
    A. 1
    B. 2
    C. 3
    D. 4

20. The gauge box is used for measuring the dry volume of a concrete mix. If the gauge box is to have a volume of 1 cubic yard, dimension H must be *approximately* _____ feet.
    A. 2.39
    B. 1.69
    C. 1.45
    D. .63

21. After a wedge-shaped hole has been cut into the large stone, the three-legged lifting device is inserted to lift the stone. The CORRECT order for inserting the three legs is
    A. 1, 2, 3
    B. 3, 2, 1
    C. 2, 3, 1
    D. 1, 3, 2

22. Brushes which have been used to apply shellac are BEST cleaned with
    A. alcohol         B. water
    C. carbon tetrachloride    D. acetic acid

23. When opening an emergency exit door set in the sidewalk, from inside the subway, the door should be raised slowly to avoid
    A. a sudden rush of air from the street
    B. making unnecessary noise
    C. damage to the sidewalk
    D. injuring pedestrians

24. When timbers are bolted together, a flat washer is *generally* used under the head of the bolt to
    A. prevent the bolt from turning
    B. increase the strength of the bolt
    C. reduce crushing of the wood when the bolt is tightened
    D. make it easier to turn the bolt

25. If one pipe outlet of a cross is closed with a plug, then the number of remaining outlets in the cross is
    A. 4    B. 3    C. 2    D. 1

## KEY (CORRECT ANSWERS)

1. D
2. C
3. A
4. C
5. C

6. D
7. A
8. B
9. A
10. A

11. C
12. B
13. C
14. D
15. A

16. B
17. B
18. D
19. D
20. B

21. D
22. A
23. D
24. C
25. C

# TEST 2

DIRECTIONS: Each question or incomplete statement is followed by several suggested answers or completions. Select the one that BEST answers the question or completes the statement. *PRINT THE LETTER OF THE CORRECT ANSWER IN THE SPACE AT THE RIGHT.*

1. The MOST important reason for roping off a work area on a subway station is to    1.____

   A. protect the public
   B. protect the repair crew
   C. prevent distraction of the crew by the public
   D. prevent delays to the public

2. Shoes which have sponge rubber soles should NOT be worn around a work area because such a sole    2.____

   A. will wear quickly
   B. is not waterproof
   C. does not keep the feet warm
   D. is easily puncutred by steel objects

3. A claw hammer is *property* used for    3.____

   A. driving a cold chisel
   B. driving brads
   C. setting rivets
   D. flattening a 1/4" metal bar

4. It is POOR practice to hold a piece of wood in the hands or lap when tightening a screw in the wood because    4.____

   A. sufficient leverage cannot be obtained
   B. the screwdriver may bend
   C. the wood will probably split
   D. personal injury is likely to result

5. Open-end wrenches are made with the sides of the jaws at about a 15-degree angle to the line of the handle. This angle    5.____

   A. is useful when working the wrench in close quarters
   B. increases the strength of the jaws
   C. prevents extending the handle with a piece of pipe
   D. serves only to improve the appearance of the wrench

6. It is BEST to cut a piece of sheet metal with a pair of snips by starting each cut with the metal sheet    6.____

   A. out near the points of the snips
   B. as far back in the jaws as possible
   C. midway between the snip points and the pivot
   D. 1/4 the way between the snip points and the pivot

7. Asphalt is a material which is used for

    A. brick reinforcement
    B. increasing the strength of poured concrete
    C. fireproofing
    D. water-proofing

8. Cement-lined drain pipe should be cut with a

    A. chisel  B. file  C. star drill  D. hacksaw

9. A riser is *generally* a pipe run which is

    A. horizontal
    B. curved
    C. vertical
    D. at a 45 degree angle

10. A lead ribbon gasket is sometimes employed when mounting and fastening enamel sign plates. This is *probably* to prevent

    A. corrosion
    B. electrolysis
    C. chipping
    D. discoloration

11. The load of a foundation is transmitted through a supporting structure to a lower level by means of

    A. underpinning
    B. framing
    C. bonding
    D. levelling

12. Back-pressure valves are provided in the connections between subway drain pipes and the city sewer system to

    A. equalize drain pipe and sewer pressure
    B. insure water flow from the sewer to the drain pipe
    C. prevent water from the sewer system from going into the drain pipe
    D. provide pressure to enable the water to flow in either direction

13. A non-rising stem type gate valve is *especially* useful where

    A. the stem must move downward only
    B. the pressure in the pipe must remain constant
    C. clearances around the valve are limited
    D. hand control of the valve is not required

14. Ferrules or sleeves in the walls and roof of the subway structure are provided for

    A. insulating the structure from the ground
    B. water pipes which pass through the structure
    C. reinforcing the concrete
    D. cooling the concrete while it is setting

15. Hair felt is commonly used for

    A. heat insulation
    B. electrical insulation
    C. grouting
    D. reinforcement

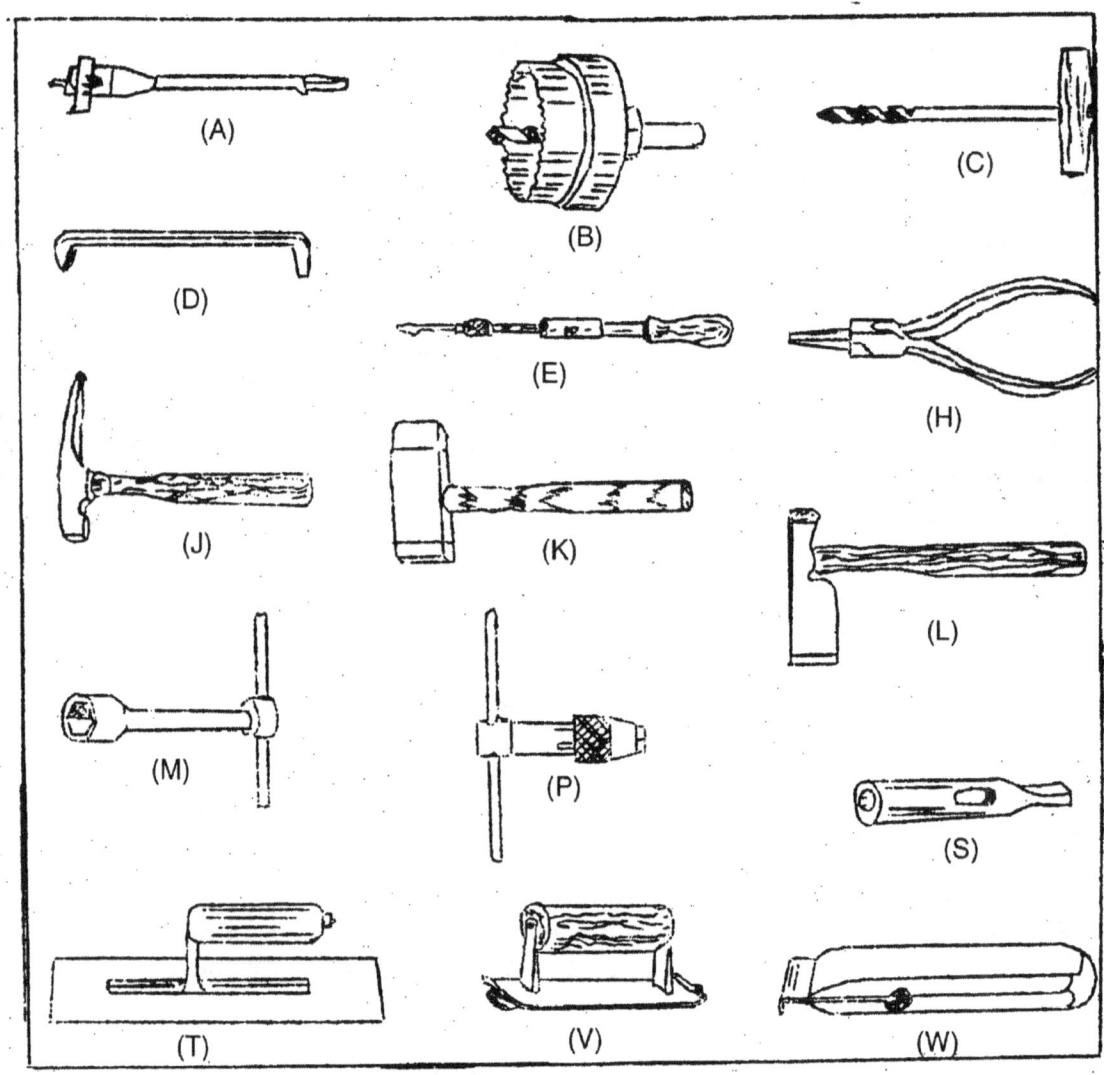

QUESTIONS 16-25.

Questions 16-25 refer to the use of the tools shown above. Read the item, and for the operation given, select the proper tool to be used from those shown.

16. Turning a screw tap when threading a hole in a steel block.  16.____

17. Boring a number of different diameter holes through a heavy wood plank.  17.____

18. Quickly screwing a number of wood screws into a board.  18.____

19. Setting a groove in a cement floor before hardening of the cement.  19.____

20. Plastering a wall.  20.____

21. Chipping a small piece out of a brick to clear a projecting steel rod, when building a brick wall.  21.____

22. Tightening a large nut.  22.____

4 (#2)

23. Quickly boring a small hole through a 1/8" board. 23.____

24. Unfastening wood screws located in a position inaccessible to an ordinary screwdriver. 24.____

25. Making a 1 1/2" hole in a steel plate. 25.____

---

# KEY (CORRECT ANSWERS)

1. A
2. D
3. B
4. D
5. A

6. B
7. D
8. D
9. C
10. C

11. A
12. C
13. C
14. B
15. A

16. P
17. A
18. E
19. V
20. T

21. J
22. M
23. C
24. D
25. B

---

# TEST 3

DIRECTIONS: Each question or incomplete statement is followed by several suggested answers or completions. Select the one that BEST answers the question or completes the Statement. *PRINT THE LETTER OF THE CORRECT ANSWER IN THE SPACE AT THE RIGHT.*

1. When holes in structural steel are reamed, it *generally* indicates that the holes are    1.____

   A. to have rough interior surface
   B. tapered
   C. to be punched after reaming
   D. to close measurement tolerances

2. A pneumatic bucker is used in    2.____

   A. riveting            B. brazing
   C. soldering           D. reinforcing concrete

3. When doing subway repair work consisting of excavating or concreting near the open ends of vent flues and pipes, these open ends are temporarily plugged to prevent    3.____

   A. noise from rising up into the street
   B. accumulation of dirt and debris in the pipes and flues
   C. drafts of cold air from bothering the repair crew
   D. fumes from rising to the street

4. Drain pipes are tested by passing a hardwood ball, smaller than the inside diameter of the pipe, through the pipe. If the hardwood ball is fractured on passing through the pipe, it *probably* means that the    4.____

   A. drain pipe has satisfactory strength
   B. ball is defective
   C. inside diameter of the pipe is too large
   D. pipe is unsatisfactory

5. Whenever a subway duct line containing electric cables is to be broken away, the work must be done with hand tools, and NOT with power equipment, because    5.____

   A. less time is required with hand tools
   B. there is less chance of damaging the cables
   C. hand tools are insulated
   D. too much power would be required for the power tools

6. Before laying concrete on an earth surface, it is GOOD practice to    6.____

   A. wet down and ram the earth
   B. thoroughly dry the earth
   C. loosen the earth thoroughly
   D. place a canvas between the earth and the poured concrete

7. Troweling the top surface of poured concrete    7.____

   A. weakens the concrete
   B. introduces dirt into the concrete

C. helps to make it waterproof
D. makes the concrete more flexible

8. A piece of new structural steel is to be riveted to a piece of old structural steel which is already drilled and in place. In this case, it is BEST to drill the matching holes in the new steel

   A. before delivery to the work location
   B. at the work location
   C. larger than those in the existing steel
   D. smaller than those in the existing steel

8._____

9. To remove a formed rivet from a steel column, it is *generally* preferable to cut or knock off the head of the rivet rather than burn it out with a torch. This is *mainly* because the torch

   A. will burn the steel and distort the rivet hole
   B. causes unpleasant fumes
   C. is expensive to use
   D. damages the rivet to be removed

9._____

10. To make certain two points separated by a vertical distance! of 8 feet are in perfect vertical alignment, it would be BEST to use a

    A. surface gage
    B. height gage
    C. protractor
    D. plumb bob

10._____

11. When repair work is being done on the elevated structure, canvas spreads are suspended under the working area *mainly* to

    A. reduce noise
    B. discourage crowds
    C. protect the structure
    D. protect pedestrians

11._____

12. If the piece of sheet metal is to be cylindrically formed into a hand scoop by soldering edges X and Y together, then the resultant scoop will be No.

    A. 1
    B. 2
    C. 3
    D. 4

12._____

13. If the subway wall tile panel is to be completed using the pattern shown, which is made up of three different sized tiles, then the additional number of tiles required for completion is
    A. 8
    B. 10
    C. 12
    D. 14

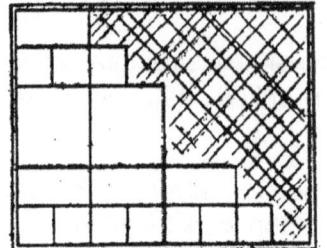
SUBWAY WALL TILE PANEL

14. The thin sheet piece when properly folded will form a closed box with a square top and bottom. Dimension Z of the box will be
    A. 2
    B. 4
    C. 6
    D. 8

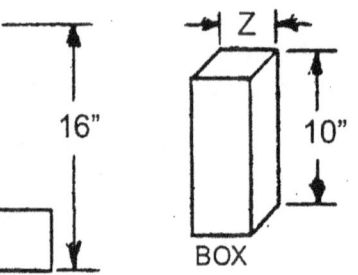

15. In the wood frame shown, whose corners are all square, the TOTAL length of one inch board is _____ inches.
    A. 40
    B. 42
    C. 44
    D. 46

16. A piece is to be cut out of the angle iron in order to make the right angle bracket shown. Angle X should be _____ degrees.
    A. 40
    B. 55
    C. 75
    D. 90

QUESTIONS 17-25.

Questions 17-25 are based solely on the instructions for carpentry work on elevated stations as given below. Read these instructions carefully before answering these items.

### CARPENTRY WORK ON ELEVATED STATIONS

Joists are to be 3 inches by 10 inches and bridging shall be 2 inches by 4 inches. All joists are to be yellow pine, spaced 20 inches on centers. Joists having a span of from 8 feet to 16 feet are to have one row of cross bridging while spans of over 16 feet are to have two rows of cross bridging. Bridging shall be nailed at each end. The joists are fastened to the steel supporting beams with special clips. Wood flooring for train platforms is to be yellow pine, 2 inches by 6 inches, dressed four sides, laid transversely with 1/4-inch open joints and is not to be used in lengths of less than five feet. Service walks (track walks) are to consist of five lengths of slatting laid side by side and continuously. The slatting is to be 2 inches by 6 inches and of random lengths varying upward in multiples of four feet six inches. Slatting is to be fastened to each support by two twenty penny cut nails.

17. Joists are fastened to the supporting beams with 17.____

    A. special clips              B. ordinary nails
    C. twenty penny nails         D. screws

18. Slatting may be used without cutting, if it has a length of 18.____

    A. 4 feet                     B. 4 feet 5 inches
    C. 9 feet                     D. 12 feet

19. Joists shall be 19.____

    A. 3" x 5" yellow pine        B. 3" x 10" yellow pine
    C. 3" x 6" spruce             D. 2" x 8" spruce

20. Wood which is dressed four sides is used for 20.____

    A. bridging                   B. joists
    C. service walks              D. train platform flooring

21. The center spacing of joists is to be 21.____

    A. 15 inches                  B. 20 inches
    C. 5 feet 4 inches            D. 7 feet

22. The number of rows of cross bridging required for joists having a span of 18 feet is 22.____

    A. four        B. three        C. two        D. one

23. Slatting is fastened 23.____

    A. to every other joist       B. with ten penny nails
    C. to each support            D. with special clips

24. Service walks are to have a width of _____ slats. 24.____

    A. 3           B. 4            C. 5          D. 6

25. Wood which is to be 2" x 6" is for 25.____

    A. platform flooring and the track walks
    B. the bridging *only*
    C. the track walks and the joists
    D. platform flooring and the bridging

## KEY (CORRECT ANSWERS)

1. D
2. A
3. B
4. D
5. B

6. A
7. C
8. B
9. A
10. D

11. D
12. A
13. C
14. B
15. C

16. D
17. A
18. C
19. B
20. D

21. B
22. C
23. C
24. C
25. A

---

# TEST 4

DIRECTIONS: Each question or incomplete statement is followed by several suggested answers or completions. Select the one that BEST answers the question or completes the Statement. *PRINT THE LETTER OF THE CORRECT ANSWER IN THE SPACE AT THE RIGHT.*

1. The angle iron is to be cut and bent into the shape shown. Assuming all approximately right angle corners in the final shape, the MINIMUM number of pieces which must be cut from the angle iron is
    A. 7
    B. 5
    C. 3
    D. 2

   1.____

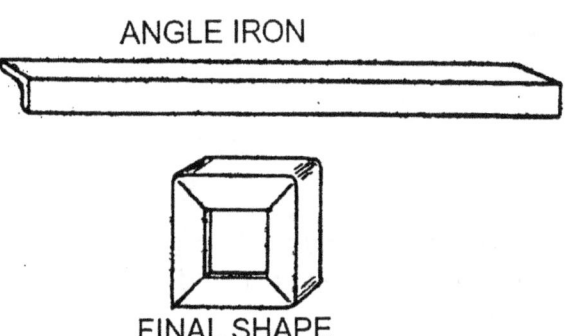

2. The wood joint which is a mortise and tenon is No.
    A. 1
    B. 2
    C. 3
    D. 4

   2.____

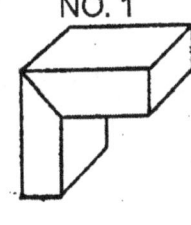 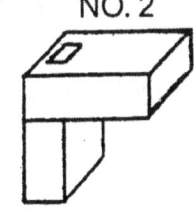

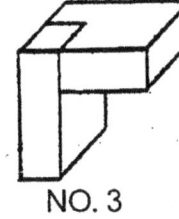 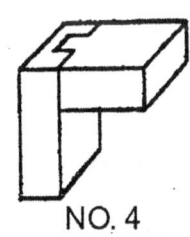

3. On the curved metal sheet, the distance X is _____ inches.
    A. 6
    B. 4
    C. 3
    D. 2

   3.____

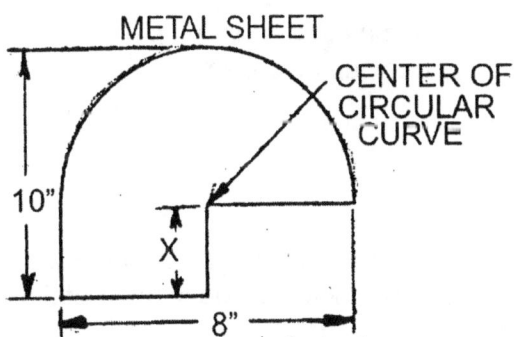

4. Tongue and groove flooring is shown in sketch No.
   A. 1
   B. 2
   C. 3
   D. 4

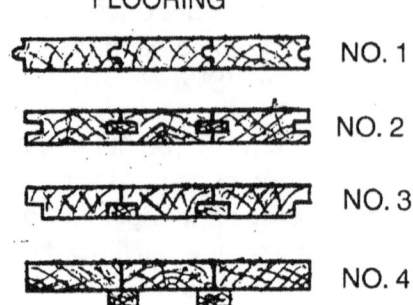

5. The pipe fitting required for connecting the 1 inch pipe to the one and a half inch valve is a
   A. close nipple
   B. street ell
   C. reducing bushing
   D. reducing coupling

6. The MAXIMUM number of 2 inch by 3 inch rectangular pieces which can be cut from the metal sheet is
   A. 8
   B. 6
   C. 4
   D. 2

7. The U-bend in the sink drain pipe is *mainly* for the purpose of preventing
   A. water leakage
   B. waste back-up
   C. hammer noise in the pipe
   D. back-up of foul air

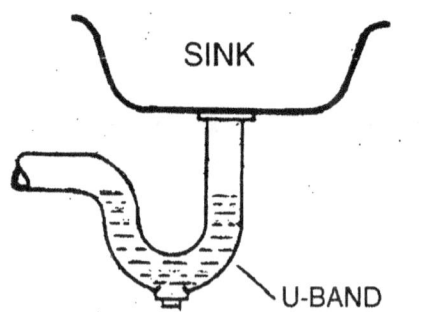

8. The distance X between the centers of the 1/2 inch holes drilled in the metal bar is _____ inches.
   A. 8 3/4
   B. 6 1/4
   C. 6 3/4
   D. 3 3/4

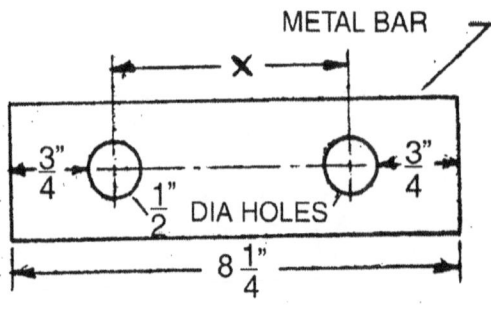

9. The cap screw which is specifically designed for a counterboard hole is No.
   A. 1
   B. 2
   C. 3
   D. 4

   CAP SCREWS
   NO. 1   NO. 2   NO. 3   NO. 4

10. When the joist hanger is used, the joists and girder are fitted together
    A. by notching the joists *only*
    B. by notching the girder *only*
    C. by notching both the joists and the girder
    D. without notching either the joists or girder

11. *Generally,* water supply pipes running outside the subway structure which are located less than four feet below a street are covered with insulating material to protect them from
    A. street heat
    B. high voltage
    C. freezing
    D. vibration

12. Machine bolts and screws which are stored or to be sent in shipment sometimes have the threads covered with graphite to
    A. strengthen the threads
    B. soften the threads
    C. prevent corrosion of the threads
    D. identify the shipment

13. When grinding a weld smooth, it is MOST important to avoid
    A. overheating the surrounding metal
    B. grinding too much of the weld away
    C. grinding too slowly
    D. grinding after the weld has cooled off

14. Steel rods or wire mesh used to reinforce concrete should be
    A. mounted firmly in the desired position before pouring the concrete
    B. made of rust-proof steel only
    C. mounted loosely to allow for movement while pouring the concrete
    D. dropped into the concrete after it has been poured

15. Wood is LEAST likely to split when a nail is driven through it if the wood

    A. is very thin
    B. is very hard
    C. has been bleached white by the sun
    D. is soft

16. Cadmium plating is applied to iron brackets and hangars after the parts have been drilled. The reason for plating after drilling is

    A. to protect the inside surfaces of the holes
    B. to avoid the safety hazard in drilling cadmium materials
    C. that the plating makes the metal too hard to drill
    D. to save plating material

17. A gouge is a tool used for

    A. planing wood smooth
    B. grinding metal
    C. drilling steel
    D. chiseling wood

18. Copper flashing is *usually* installed in the roof of a building to

    A. make it fireproof
    B. insulate it against lightning discharge
    C. ventilate the roof area
    D. prevent roof leaks at certain points

19. Newly installed underground pipes which must pass a pressure test are left exposed until they have passed the test to

    A. avoid dirt blow-ups in case of leaks
    B. see if the pipes move under pressure
    C. spot bulges in the pipe
    D. make it easier to spot leaks and make repairs

20. Proper setting and hardening of poured concrete depends on weather conditions. It would be CORRECT to state that concrete which is hardening is

    A. never covered in any kind of weather
    B. kept wet by sprinkling during hot weather
    C. kept below 40° F. during hot weather
    D. covered with a water layer during freezing weather

21. Steel helmets give workers the MOST protection from

    A. falling objects
    B. eye injuries
    C. fire
    D. electric shock

22. It is POOR practice to wear goggles when

    A. chipping stone
    B. using a grinder
    C. climbing or descending ladders
    D. handling molten metal

23. When using a brace and bit to bore a hole completely through a partition, it is MOST important to

    A. lean heavily on the brace and bit
    B. maintain a steady turning speed all through the job
    C. have the body in a position that will not be easily thrown off balance
    D. reverse the direction of the bit at frequent intervals

23.____

24. One advantage of plywood is that is

    A. is cheaper than soft pine
    B. does not contain any glue
    C. never splinters
    D. resists warping

24.____

25. Gloves should be used when handling

    A. lanterns
    B. wooden rules
    C. heavy ropes
    D. all small tools

25.____

# KEY (CORRECT ANSWERS)

| | | | |
|---|---|---|---|
| 1. | B | 11. | C |
| 2. | B | 12. | C |
| 3. | A | 13. | B |
| 4. | A | 14. | A |
| 5. | C | 15. | D |
| 6. | B | 16. | A |
| 7. | D | 17. | D |
| 8. | B | 18. | D |
| 9. | B | 19. | D |
| 10. | D | 20. | B |

21. A
22. C
23. C
24. D
25. C

# EXAMINATION SECTION
## TEST 1

DIRECTIONS: Each question or incomplete statement is followed by several suggested answers or completions. Select the one that BEST answers the question or completes the statement. *PRINT THE LETTER OF THE CORRECT ANSWER IN THE SPACE AT THE RIGHT.*

1. Employees should be familiar with the rules and regulations governing their jobs *mainly* to

    A. eliminate overtime
    B. justify mistakes
    C. pass promotion examinations
    D. perform their duties properly

2. When summoning an ambulance for an injured person, it is MOST important to give the

    A. name of the injured person
    B. nature of the injuries
    C. cause of the accident
    D. location of the injured person

3. The *most likely* cause of accidents involving minor injuries is

    A. careless work practices
    B. lack of safety devices
    C. inferior equipment and material
    D. insufficient safety posters

4. When you are newly assigned as a helper to an experienced maintainer, he is *most likely* to give you good training if your attitude is that

    A. he is responsible for your progress
    B. you have the basic knowledge but lack the details
    C. you need the benefit of his experience
    D. he should do the jobs where little is to be learned

5. A sheet metal plate has been cut in the form of a right triangle with sides of 5, 12, and 13 inches. The area of this plate is, in square inches,

    A. 30      B. 32 1/2      C. 60      D. 78

6. The side support for steps or stairs is called a

    A. ledger board      B. runner
    C. stringer          D. riser

7. In an accident report, the information which may be MOST useful in DECREASING the recurrence of similar type accidents is the

    A. extent of injuries sustained
    B. time the accident happened
    C. number of people involved
    D. cause of the accident

8. The circumference of a circle is given by the formula C = πD, where C is the circumference, D is the diameter and π is about 3 1/7. If a coil of 15 turns of steel cable has an average diameter of 20 inches, the TOTAL length of cable, in feet, on the coil is NEAREST to

    A. 5   B. 78   C. 550   D. 943

9. In order to determine if a surface is truly horizontal, it should be checked with a

    A. carpenter's square
    B. plumb bob
    C. steel rule
    D. spirit level

10. A steel beam that is supported at one end on a masonry wall will *generally* be provided with a steel bearing plate under this end in order to

    A. protect the beam from any corrosive action of the masonry
    B. prevent the wall from being injured by any failure of the beam
    C. spread the load from the beam over a wider area of the wall
    D. prevent any rocking motion of the beam on the wall

11. Before a newly riveted connection can be approved, the rivets should be struck with a light hammer in order to

    A. improve the shape of the rivet heads
    B. knock off any rust or burnt metal
    C. detect any loose rivets
    D. give the rivets a tighter fit

12. Wall sheathing can be installed either diagonally or horizontally on the studs. When installed diagonally, the wall is

    A. cheaper
    B. smoother
    C. more weatherproof
    D. more rigid

13. The measurements of a poured concrete foundation shows that 54 cubic feet of concrete have been placed. If payment for this concrete is to be on the basic of cubic yards, the 54 cubic feet must be

    A. multiplied by 27
    B. multiplied by 3
    C. divided by 27
    D. divided by 3

14. The two materials which have been used to the GREATEST extent for the construction of the subway system are

    A. brick and steel
    B. steel and concrete
    C. wood and steel
    D. wood and concrete

15. The spacing along the track from one subway column to the next is *generally* about _____ feet.

    A. 2   B. 5   C. 25   D. 50

QUESTIONS 16-25.

Questions 16 to 25 inclusive in Column I are articles or terms used in structure maintenance and repair work, each of which is associated *primarily* (though not exclusively) with one of the trade specialties listed in Column II. For each article or term in Column I, select the trade specialty from Column II in which it is in greatest use. Indicate in the correspondingly numbered row the letter preceding your selected trade specialty.

| | Column I<br>(Articles or Terms) | | Column II<br>(Trade Specialities) | |
|---|---|---|---|---|
| 16. | Drift pin | A. | Carpentry | 16.____ |
| 17. | Studding | B. | Masonry | 17.____ |
| 18. | Elbow | C. | Ironwork | 18.____ |
| 19. | Header course | D. | Plumbing | 19.____ |
| 20. | Dowel | | | 20.____ |
| 21. | Screeding | | | 21.____ |
| 22. | Cleanout | | | 22.____ |
| 23. | Air jam | | | 23.____ |
| 24. | Curing | | | 24.____ |
| 25. | Mortise and tenon | | | 25.____ |

## KEY (CORRECT ANSWERS)

| | | | | |
|---|---|---|---|---|
| 1. | D | | 11. | C |
| 2. | D | | 12. | D |
| 3. | A | | 13. | C |
| 4. | C | | 14. | B |
| 5. | A | | 15. | B |
| 6. | C | | 16. | C |
| 7. | D | | 17. | A |
| 8. | B | | 18. | D |
| 9. | D | | 19. | B |
| 10. | C | | 20. | A |

| | |
|---|---|
| 21. | B |
| 22. | D |
| 23. | C |
| 24. | B |
| 25. | A |

# TEST 2

DIRECTIONS: Each question or incomplete statement is followed by several suggested answers or completions. Select the one that BEST answers the question or completes the statement. *PRINT THE LETTER OF THE CORRECT ANSWER IN THE SPACE AT THE RIGHT.*

1. A foreman reprimands a helper for walking across the subway tracks unnecessarily in violation of the rules and regulations. The BEST reaction of the helper in this situation is to

    A. tell the foreman that he was careful and that he did not take any chances
    B. keep quiet and accept the criticism
    C. explain that he took this action to save time
    D. demand that the foreman show him the rule he violated

2. The helper who would probably be rated HIGHEST by his supervisor is the one who

    A. listens to instruction and carries them out
    B. never lets the maintainer to whom he is assigned do any heavy lifting
    C. asks many questions about the work
    D. makes many suggestions on work procedures

3. If a co-worker is not breathing after receiving an electric shock but is no longer in contact with the electricity, it is MOST important for you to

    A. avoid moving him
    B. wrap the victim in a blanket
    C. force him to take hot liquids
    D. start artificial respiration promptly

4. Good practice requires that the end of a pipe to be installed in a plumbing system be reamed to remove the inside burr after it has been cut to length. The purpose of this reaming is to

    A. remove loose rust
    B. finish the pipe accurately to length
    C. restore the original inside diameter of the pipe at the end
    D. make the threading of the pipe easier

5. A box contains an equal number of iron and brass castings. Each iron casting weighs 2 pounds and each brass casting one pound. If the box contents weigh 240 lbs., the number of iron pieces in the box is

    A. 160        B. 120        C. 80        D. 40

6. The roofs of stations on the elevated sections of rail are *generally* covered with

    A. sheet metal              B. asbestos shingles
    C. tiles                    D. tar paper

7. Where wide train steps are provided with a center dividing railing, the railing is *usually* constructed of

    A. angle irons              B. steel pipe
    C. sheet metal panels       D. wrought iron

8. If the feet of a ladder are found to be resting on a slightly uneven surface, it would be BEST to  8.____

   A. move the ladder to an entirely different location
   B. even up the feet of the ladder with a small wedge
   C. get two men to bolster the ladder while it is being climbed
   D. get another ladder that is more suitable to the conditions

9. It would be POOR practice to hold a piece of wood in your hands or lap while you are tightening a screw in the wood because  9.____

   A. the wood would probably split
   B. sufficient leverage cannot be obtained
   C. the screwdriver may bend
   D. you might injure yourself

10. A mixture of cement, sand, and water is called  10.____

    A. hydrated lime         B. plain concrete
    C. hydrated cement       D. mortar

11. A gauge of a nail indicates the  11.____

    A. length of the shank      B. diameter of the head
    C. thickness of the head    D. diameter of the shank

12. If a man on a job has to report an accident to the office by telephone, he should request the name of the person taking the call and also note the time. The reason for this precaution is to fix responsibility for the  12.____

    A. entire handling of the accident thereafter
    B. accuracy of the report
    C. recording of the report
    D. preparation of the final written report

13. Employees of the transit system whose work requires them to enter upon the tracks in the subway are warned NOT to wear loose fitting clothes. The MOST important reason for this warning is that loose fitting clothes may  13.____

    A. tear more easily than snug fitting clothes
    B. give insufficient protection against subway dust
    C. catch on some projection of a passing train
    D. interfere when the men are using heavy tools

14. An effective material frequently used for preserving wood from weathering and decay is  14.____

    A. creosote        B. zinc chloride
    C. spelter         D. pumice

15. The MOST important reason for roping off a work area on a subway station is to  15.____

    A. prevent transit delays
    B. protect the public
    C. protect the work gang
    D. prevent the work gang from being distracted by the public

16. Shoes with sponge rubber soles should NOT be worn in working areas *mainly* because they

   A. are not waterproof
   B. are easily punctured by steel objects
   C. do not keep the feet warm
   D. wear out too quickly

16.___

17. The area (in square inches) of the plate shown is

17.___

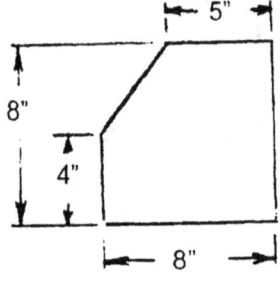

   A. 32    B. 52    C. 58    D. 64

18. In the wood frame shown, whose corners are all square, the total length of one-inch board is _____ inches.

18.___

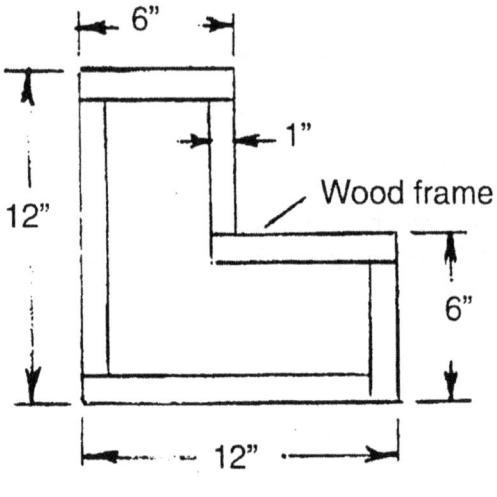

   A. 42    B. 43    C. 44    D. 45

42

4 (#2)

19. On the curved metal sheet, the distance X is, in inches,  19._____

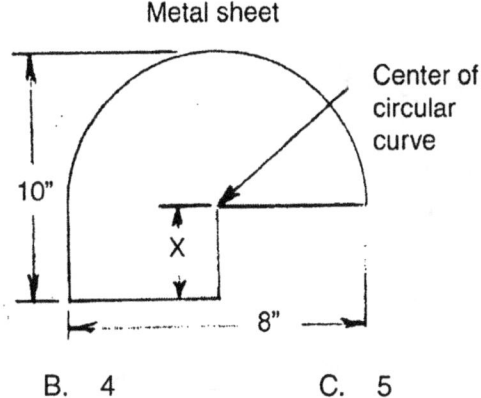

A. 3  B. 4  C. 5  D. 6

20. The number of feet of wire fencing needed to divide the area shown into four completely fenced-in square sections, all equal in area, would be  20._____

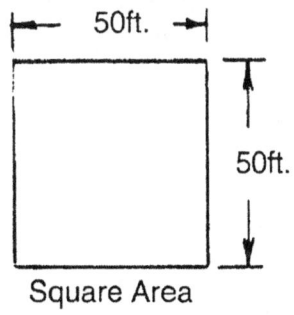

Square Area

A. 2500  B. 300  C. 200  D. 100

21. When floor beams are to be supported by nailing to vertical supports, then the STRONGEST arrangement would be provided by the method shown in sketch No.  21._____

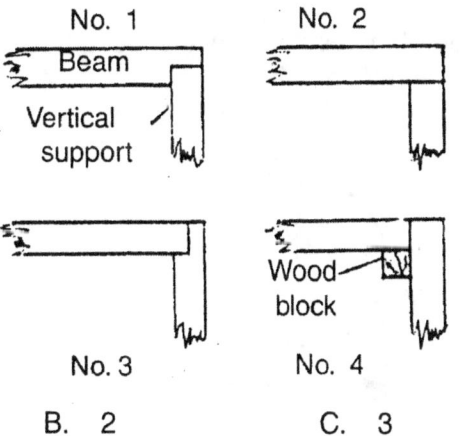

A. 1  B. 2  C. 3  D. 4

43

22. The weight "W" is to be raised as shown by attaching the pull rope to a truck. If the weight is to be raised 8 feet, the truck will have to move _____ feet.  22._____

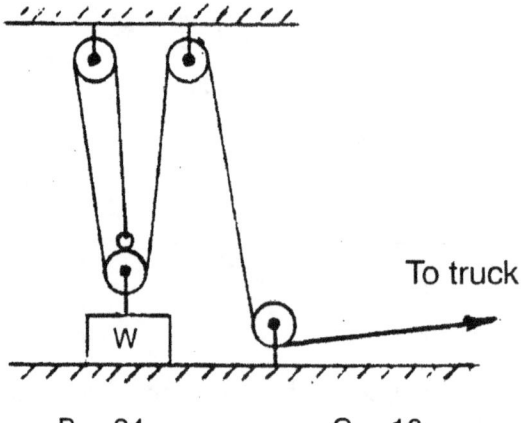

   A. 32  B. 24  C. 16  D. 8

23. Four plots of ground of equal area are as shown. It is proposed to use chain-link fencing to fence in the four plots. The LEAST amount of fencing would be needed for plot No.  23._____

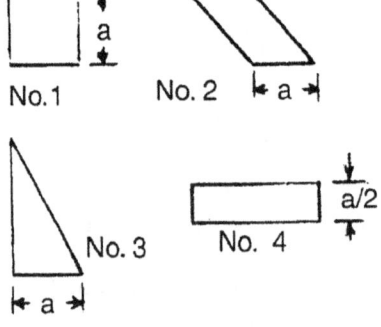

   A. 1  B. 2  C. 3  D. 4

24. The area of the shaded portion of the circle shown is found by multiplying one-fourth of the square of the diameter, D, by 22/7 and by  24._____

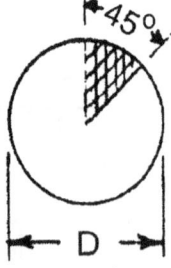

   A. 1/8  B. 1/6  C. 1/4  D. 1/3

25. The open-top tin box shown at the right can be made by bending along the dotted lines of the flat cut sheet marked   25._____

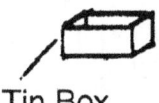
Tin Box

A.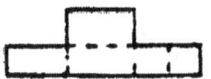

B.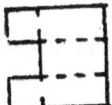

C.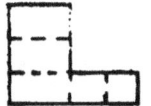

D.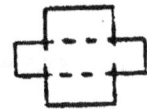

## KEY (CORRECT ANSWERS)

| | | | |
|---|---|---|---|
| 1. | B | 11. | D |
| 2. | A | 12. | C |
| 3. | D | 13. | C |
| 4. | C | 14. | A |
| 5. | C | 15. | B |
| 6. | A | 16. | B |
| 7. | B | 17. | C |
| 8. | B | 18. | C |
| 9. | D | 19. | D |
| 10. | D | 20. | B |

| | |
|---|---|
| 21. | B |
| 22. | B |
| 23. | A |
| 24. | A |
| 25. | D |

# TEST 3

DIRECTIONS: Each question or incomplete statement is followed by several suggested answers or completions. Select the one that BEST answers the question or completes the statement. *PRINT THE LETTER OF THE CORRECT ANSWER IN THE SPACE AT THE RIGHT.*

1. In MOST cases, the logical and proper source from which you should FIRST seek explanation of a transit rule you do not understand would be the   1.____

    A. helper who has an assignment similar to yours
    B. maintainer with whom you are assigned to work
    C. head of your department
    D. transit authority

2. In case of accident, employees who witnessed the accident are required by the rules to make individual written reports on prescribed forms as soon as possible. The MOST logical reason for requiring such individual reports rather than a single joint report signed by all witnesses is that the individual reports are   2.____

    A. *less* likely to be lost at the same time
    B. *more* likely to result in reducing the number of accidents
    C. *less* likely to contain unnecessary information
    D. *more* likely to give the complete picture

3. The pipe that is MOST likely to break if it is dropped is one made from   3.____

    A. soft steel             B. wrought iron
    C. aluminum               D. cast iron

4. A nominal 6" x 8" wood timber as normally obtained is *actually*   4.____

    A. a full 6" thick and a full 8" deep
    B. more than 6" thick and more than 8" deep
    C. less than 6" thick and less than 8" deep
    D. more than 6" thick but less than 8" deep

5. A serious safety hazard occurs when a   5.____

    A. hardened steel hammer is used to strike a hardened steel surface
    B. soft iron hammer is used to strike a hardened steel surface
    C. hardened steel hammer is used to strike a soft iron surface
    D. soft iron hammer is used to strike a soft iron surface

6. When an emergency exit door set in the sidewalk is being opened from inside the subway, the door should be opened slowly to avoid   6.____

    A. injury to pedestrian
    B. making unnecessary noise
    C. a sudden rush of air from the street
    D. damage to the sidewalk

7. The MAIN purpose of the periodic inspections of transit facilities and equipment that are made by the maintainers is *probably* to   7.____

A. encourage the men to take better care of these facilities and equipment
B. keep the maintainers busy during otherwise slack periods
C. discover minor faults before they develop into more serious conditions
D. make the men more familiar with these facilities and equipment

8. A rule of the transit system prohibits the use of transit system telephones for personal calls. The MOST important reason for this rule is that the added personal calls

    A. increase telephone maintenance
    B. require more operators
    C. tie up telephones which may be urgently needed for company business
    D. waste company time

9. Bricks are usually so placed in a brick wall that joints between bricks in any row do not line up with joints in the row immediately above and the one immediately below.
   The MAIN purpose of this staggering of bricks is to

    A. obtain a pleasing design
    B. make it easier to keep the successive rows level when laying the bricks
    C. prevent rain water from running in channels down the wall
    D. form a firmer wall

10. If you feel that one of your co-workers is not doing his share of the work, your BEST procedure is to

    A. increase your own output as a good example
    B. take no action and continue to do your job properly
    C. reduce your work output to bring this matter to a head
    D. point this out to the foreman

11. Maintenance workers of the transit system are required to report defective equipment to their superiors even when the maintenance of the particular equipment is handled by another bureau. The purpose of this rule is to

    A. reward those who keep their eyes open
    B. punish employees who do not do their jobs
    C. have repairs made before serious trouble occurs
    D. keep employees on their toes

12. When you are FIRST appointed as a helper and are assigned to work with a maintainer, he will *probably* expect you to

    A. pay close attention to instructions
    B. do very little work
    C. make plenty of mistakes
    D. do all of the unpleasant work

13. Concrete will crack MOST easily when it is subject to

    A. compression      B. bearing      C. bonding      D. tension

14. When marking and sawing a timber to a desired length, it is GOOD practice to mark

A. slightly smaller than the length and saw just outside the line on the waste side
B. the exact length and cut just outside the line on the waste side
C. the exact length and cut on the line
D. slightly larger than the length and cut on the line

15. From your knowledge and observation of the subway, the logical reason that certain employees who work on the tracks carry small parts in fiber pails rather than steel pails is that fiber pails

   A. cannot be dented by rough usage
   B. do not conduct electricity
   C. are stronger
   D. cannot rust

16. Maintenance workers whose duties require them to work on the tracks generally work in pairs. The LEAST likely of the following possible reasons for this practice is that

   A. the men can help each other in case of accident
   B. it protects against vandalism
   C. some of the work requires two men
   D. there is usually too much equipment for one man to carry

17. In order to repair a leaky faucet, it would be BEST to FIRST replace the

   A. washer    B. spindle    C. bonnet    D. seat

QUESTIONS 18-25.
Questions 18 to 25 refer to the figures below.

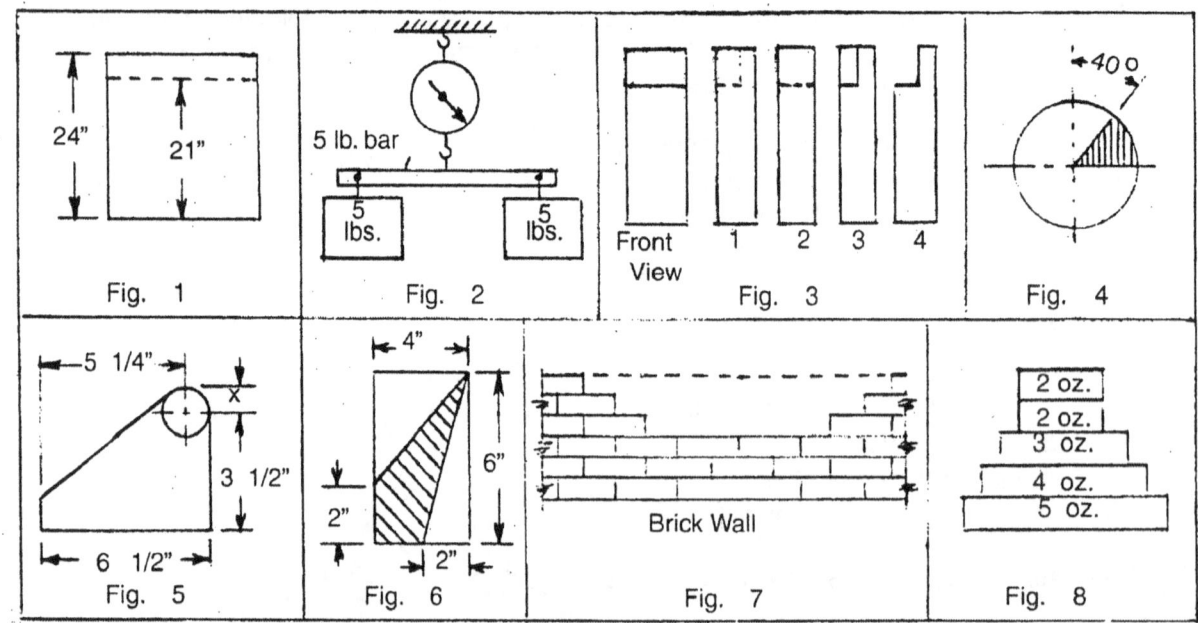

18. Fig. 1 shows a water tank having a total capacity of 120 gallons, which is partially filled. If 60 gallons are drained, the NEW water level will be

   A. 16"    B. 13"    C. 9"    D. 7"

19. In Fig. 2, which shows a balanced bar, the weighing scale will read *approximately*  19.____
    A. zero    B. 5 lbs.    C. 10 lbs.    D. 15 lbs.

20. Fig. 3 shows a front view of a steel piece. The CORRECT SIDE view is No.  20.____
    A. 1    B. 2    C. 3    D. 4

21. Fig. 4 shows a shaded sector on a circular metal sheet. The MAXIMUM number of such  21.____
    sectors which can be cut from the sheet is
    A. 7    B. 8    C. 9    D. 10

22. In Fig. 5, dimension "X" is  22.____
    A. 1 1/4"    B. 1 3/4"    C. 2"    D. 2 1/2"

23. In Fig. 6, the area in square inches of the shaded portion of the rectangle is  23.____
    A. 10    B. 14    C. 24    D. 28

24. In Fig. 7, the number of full-size bricks required to complete the brick wall to the dotted  24.____
    line is
    A. 7    B. 9    C. 12    D. 15

25. Using only the balance weights shown in Fig. 8, the LEAST number of weights needed  25.____
    for a scale requiring 3/4 pounds of weights to balance is
    A. 5    B. 4    C. 3    D. 2

---

# KEY (CORRECT ANSWERS)

| | |
|---|---|
| 1. B | 11. C |
| 2. D | 12. A |
| 3. D | 13. D |
| 4. C | 14. B |
| 5. A | 15. B |
| 6. A | 16. B |
| 7. C | 17. A |
| 8. C | 18. C |
| 9. D | 19. D |
| 10. B | 20. D |

21. A
22. A
23. A
24. C
25. C

# TEST 4

DIRECTIONS: Each question or incomplete statement is followed by several suggested answers or completions. Select the one that BEST answers the question or completes the statement. *PRINT THE LETTER OF THE CORRECT ANSWER IN THE SPACE AT THE RIGHT.*

1. The MAIN reason for not permitting more than one person to work on a ladder at the same time is that

   A. the ladder might get overloaded
   B. several persons on the ladder might obstruct each other
   C. time would be lost going up and down the ladder
   D. several persons could not all face the ladder at one time

   1._____

2. Safety on the job is BEST assured by

   A. keeping alert
   B. working only with new tools
   C. working very slowly
   D. avoiding the necessity for working overtime

   2._____

3. The structural steel member that is used to support a wall over a door or window opening is called a

   A. sill    B. lintel    C. stud    D. plate

   3._____

4. A mixture of cement and water is referred to as _____ cement.

   A. neat    B. Portland    C. fine    D. hydrated

   4._____

5. To secure the proper angle for resting a 12-foot ladder against a wall, the ladder should be so inclined that the distance between the bottom of the ladder and the wall is _____ feet.

   A. 2    B. 3    C. 4    D. 5

   5._____

QUESTIONS 6-25.
Questions 6-25 refer to the use of tools shown below. Refer to these tools when answering these questions.

2 (#4)

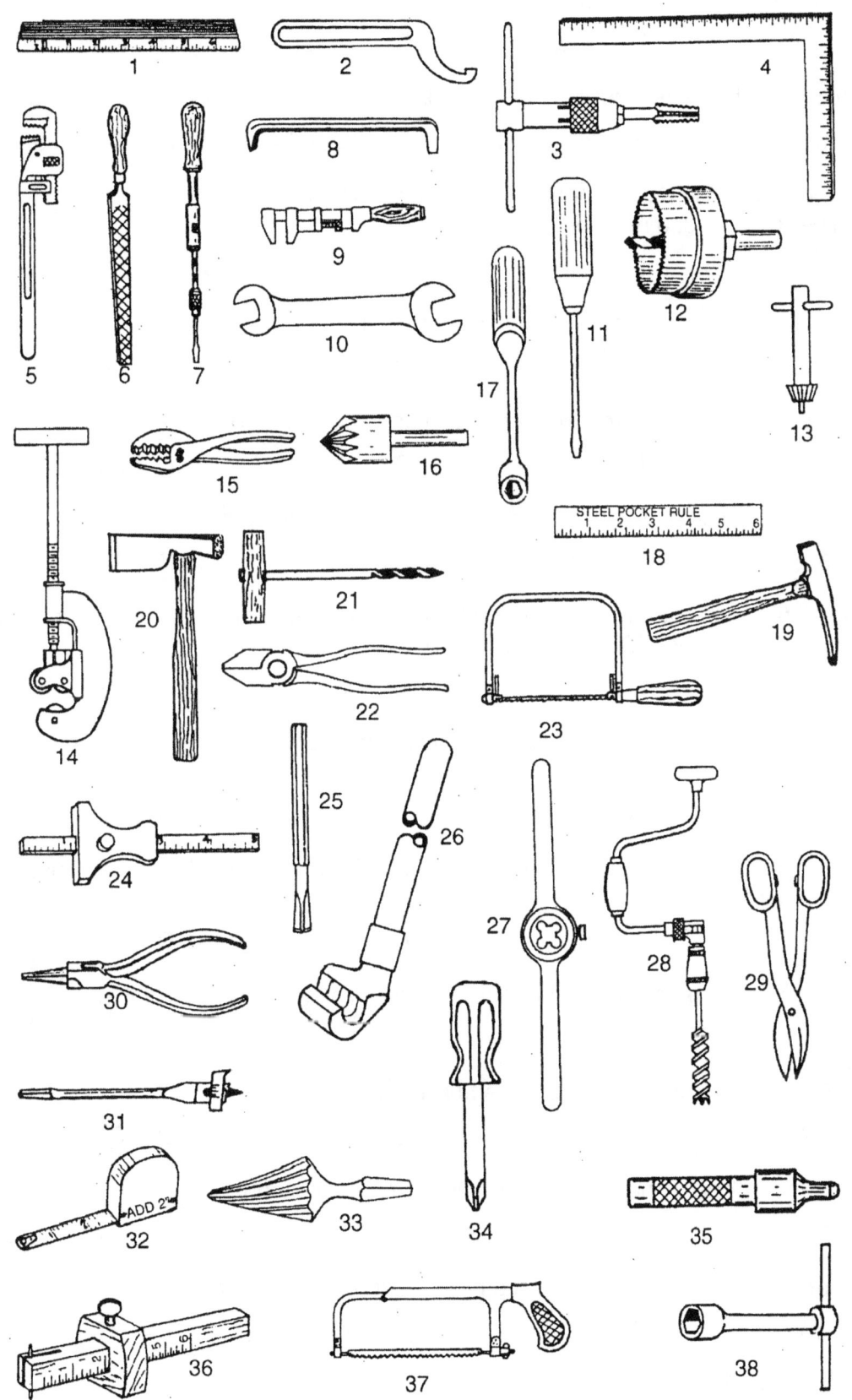

6. Tool number 38 is properly called a(n) _____ wrench.
   A. box   B. open-end   C. socket   D. tool

7. Two tools which are used for cutting large circular holes in thin sheets are numbers
   A. 12 and 31   B. 28 and 33   C. 12 and 28   D. 31 and 33

8. If there is a possible danger of electric shock when you are taking measurements, it would be BEST to use number
   A. 1   B. 4   C. 18   D. 32

9. A 1/2-inch steel pipe is *preferably* cut with number
   A. 14   B. 23   C. 27   D. 29

10. A nut for a #8 machine screw should be tightened using number
    A. 9   B. 15   C. 17   D. 38

11. The hexagon nut for a 1/2-inch diameter machine bolt should be tightened using number
    A. 5   B. 10   C. 22   D. 26

12. If a small piece must be chipped off a brick in order to clear an obstruction when a brick wall is being built, the MOST suitable tool to use is number
    A. 16   B. 19   C. 20   D. 33

13. A large number of wood screws can be screwed into a board MOST quickly by using number
    A. 7   B. 8   C. 11   D. 17

14. A number of different diameter holes can be MOST easily bored through a heavy wood plank by using number
    A. 3   B. 13   C. 21   D. 31

15. The tool to use in order to form threads in a hole in a steel block is number
    A. 2   B. 3   C. 27   D. 31

16. Curved designs in thin wood are *preferably* cut with number
    A. 12   B. 23   C. 29   D. 37

17. The driving of Phillips-head screws requires the use of number
    A. 7   B. 8   C. 11   D. 34

18. In order to properly flare one end of a piece of copper tubing, the tool to use is number
    A. 13   B. 25   C. 33   D. 35

19. Tool number 16 is used for
    A. counterboring   B. cutting concrete
    C. countersinking   D. reaming

20. A tool that can be used to drill a hole in a concrete wall to install a lead anchor is number   20.____
    A. 3   B. 16   C. 21   D. 25

21. After cutting a piece of steel pipe, the burrs are BEST removed from the inside edge with number   21.____
    A. 6   B. 13   C. 16   D. 33

22. The MOST convenient tool for measuring the depth of a 1/2-inch diameter hole is number   22.____
    A. 24   B. 31   C. 32   D. 36

23. A 1" x 1" x 1/8" angle iron would *usually* be cut using number   23.____
    A. 12   B. 26   C. 29   D. 37

24. Wood screws located in positions NOT accessible to an ordinary screwdriver would be removed using number   24.____
    A. 2   B. 8   C. 13   D. 30

25. A small hole can be quickly bored through a 1/8-inch thick plywood board with number   25.____
    A. 3   B. 7   C. 21   D. 31

---

## KEY (CORRECT ANSWERS)

| | | | |
|---|---|---|---|
| 1. A | | 11. B | |
| 2. A | | 12. B | |
| 3. B | | 13. A | |
| 4. A | | 14. D | |
| 5. B | | 15. B | |
| 6. C | | 16. B | |
| 7. A | | 17. D | |
| 8. A | | 18. D | |
| 9. A | | 19. C | |
| 10. C | | 20. D | |

21. D
22. A
23. D
24. B
25. C

# EXAMINATION SECTION
## TEST 1

DIRECTIONS: Each question or incomplete statement is followed by several suggested answers or completions. Select the one that BEST answers the question or completes the Statement. *PRINT THE LETTER OF THE CORRECT ANSWER IN THE SPACE AT THE RIGHT.*

Questions 1-16.

DIRECTIONS: Questions on these tools are to be found on the following page. (These tools are not shown to scale.)

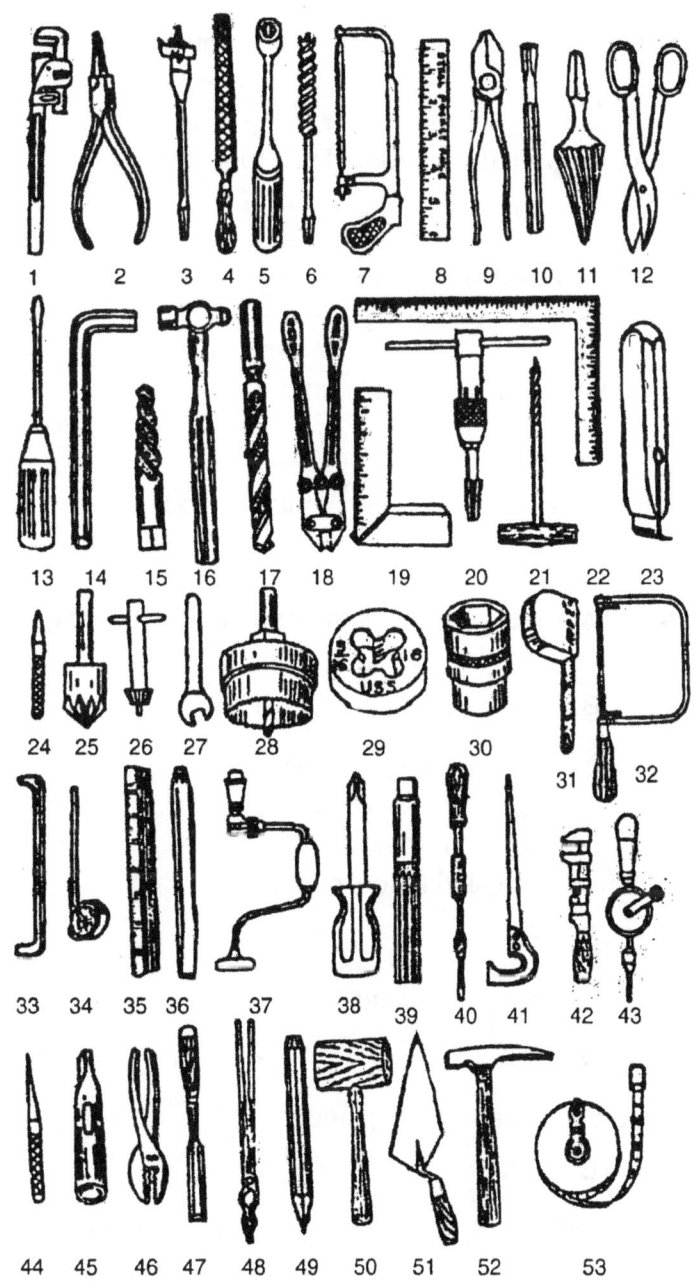

NOTE: Questions 1 through 16 refer to the tools shown on the preceding page. (The *numbers* in the choices refer to the *numbers* beneath the tools.)

1. To remove cutting burrs from the inside of a pipe, you should use tool number
    A. 4    B. 7    C. 11    D. 15

2. To join lengths of chrome-plated pipe, you should use tool
    A. 1    B. 34    C. 42    D. 46

3. To countersink a hole in a plywood shelf, you should use tool number
    A. 3    B. 11    C. 25    D. 28

4. To tighten plumbing fixtures having hexagonal ends, you should use tool number
    A. 1    B. 9    C. 34    D. 42

5. To lift a hot rivet from the furnace, you should use tool number
    A. 2    B. 18    C. 46    D. 48

6. To cut a 3/8 inch steel cable, you should use tool number
    A. 2    B. 12    C. 18    D. 41

7. To tighten a lag screw, you should use tool number
    A. 1    B. 27    C. 33    D. 46

8. To make holes for sheet metal screws, you should use tool number
    A. 3    B. 11    C. 21    D. 43

9. To remove a broken-off piece of a small-diameter pipe from a fitting, you should use tool number
    A. 11    B. 15    C. 17    D. 39

10. The term "16 oz." should be applied to tool number
    A. 1    B. 12    C. 16    D. 42

11. The term "coping" should be applied to tool number
    A. 7    B. 28    C. 32    D. 41

12. The term "die" should be applied to tool number
    A. 11    B. 20    C. 29    D. 39

13. The term "star" should be applied to tool number
    A. 3    B. 10    C. 25    D. 28

14. If tool number 6 bears the mark "5," this tool should be used to drill holes having a *diameter* of
    A. 5/32"    B. 5/16"    C. 5/8"    D. 5"

15. The marking "18" on tool number 29 refers to the   15.____

    A. maximum diameter of rod   B. minimum diameter of rod
    C. number of threads per inch   D. degree of taper of threads

16. If the marking on the blade of tool number 7 reads: "12-32," the 32 refers to the   16.____

    A. length
    B. thickness
    C. weight
    D. number of teeth per inch

17. If a maintainer is chipping concrete with a pneumatic hammer, the MOST important safety precaution for this maintainer to follow is to wear   17.____

    A. a hard hat   B. heavy shoes
    C. goggles   D. a long-sleeved shirt

18. Forms for concrete are coated with oil because the oil   18.____

    A. makes the finished surface smoother
    B. imparts a grayish color to the concrete
    C. reduces the time required for the concrete to set
    D. makes it easier to remove the forms after the concrete has set

19. Artificial respiration should be applied when an accident victim shows signs of   19.____

    A. excessive bleeding   B. rapid breathing
    C. bad scalding   D. breathing difficulties

20. Shop workers are often warned against wearing rings during working hours MAINLY because of the danger   20.____

    A. of theft   B. of loss
    C. to machinery   D. to the employee

21. The MAIN purpose of using lightweight concrete for floor construction is to   21.____

    A. improve insulation
    B. reduce the weight
    C. furnish a smooth surface
    D. make floor maintenance easier

22. The rules state that employees should not make any statements concerning transit accidents except to the proper officials. The PROBABLE reason for this rule is to   22.____

    A. prevent lawsuits
    B. keep the facts from the public
    C. avoid conflicting testimony
    D. prevent unofficial statements from being accepted as official

23. The SAFEST way of handling a bank of lights which operate on third rail power, is to   23.____

    A. connect the negative lead to the signal rail
    B. connect the negative lead to the third rail
    C. connect the positive lead before connecting the negative lead
    D. disconnect the positive lead before disconnecting the negative lead

Questions 24-31.
DIRECTIONS: In questions 24 through 31, the item referred to is shown
to the right of the question.

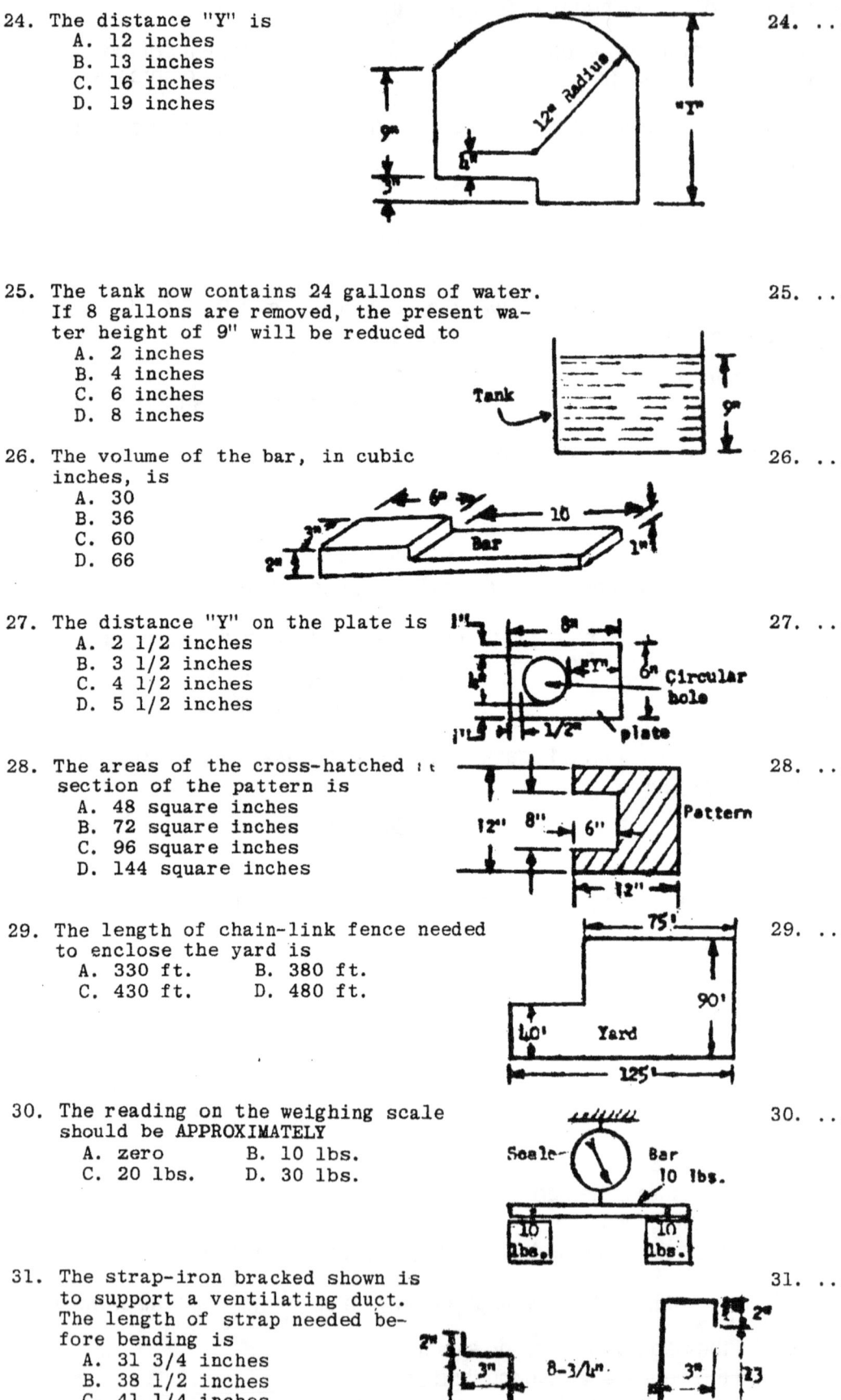

24. The distance "Y" is
    A. 12 inches
    B. 13 inches
    C. 16 inches
    D. 19 inches

25. The tank now contains 24 gallons of water.
    If 8 gallons are removed, the present water height of 9" will be reduced to
    A. 2 inches
    B. 4 inches
    C. 6 inches
    D. 8 inches

26. The volume of the bar, in cubic inches, is
    A. 30
    B. 36
    C. 60
    D. 66

27. The distance "Y" on the plate is
    A. 2 1/2 inches
    B. 3 1/2 inches
    C. 4 1/2 inches
    D. 5 1/2 inches

28. The areas of the cross-hatched section of the pattern is
    A. 48 square inches
    B. 72 square inches
    C. 96 square inches
    D. 144 square inches

29. The length of chain-link fence needed to enclose the yard is
    A. 330 ft.      B. 380 ft.
    C. 430 ft.      D. 480 ft.

30. The reading on the weighing scale should be APPROXIMATELY
    A. zero         B. 10 lbs.
    C. 20 lbs.      D. 30 lbs.

31. The strap-iron bracked shown is to support a ventilating duct.
    The length of strap needed before bending is
    A. 31 3/4 inches
    B. 38 1/2 inches
    C. 41 1/4 inches
    D. 44 1/2 inches

## 5. (#1)

Questions 32-40.
DIRECTIONS: **Questions on this plumbing sketch appear on the next page.**

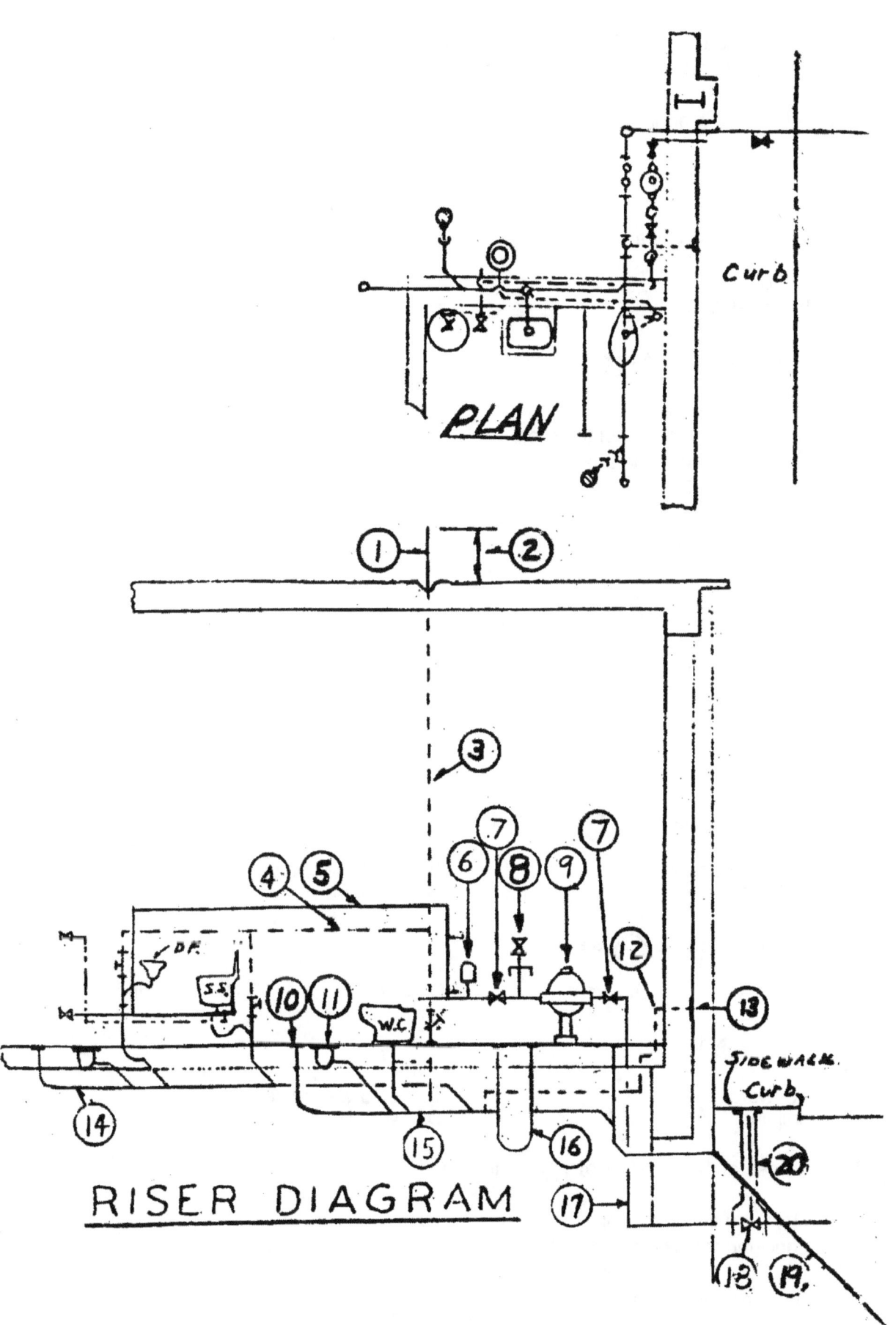

NOTE: Questions 32 through 40 refer to the plumbing sketch on the preceding page. Refer to this sketch when answering these questions.

32. The vent stack ③ should be made of

    A. cast iron
    B. galvanized iron
    C. copper
    D. plastic

33. The line marked ⑤ is a

    A. soil line
    B. vent line
    C. hot water line
    D. cold water line

34. The purpose of the valves ⑦ on either side of the meter is to

    A. reduce water hammer
    B. permit easy removal of the meter
    C. allow by-passing the meter
    D. adjust water flow

35. The purpose of the test tee at ⑧ is to

    A. determine the purity of the water
    B. establish the proper water pressure
    C. check the accuracy of the meter
    D. apply pressure to test the piping

36. The plumbing fitting in the floor at ⑩ is a

    A. trap   B. valve   C. clean out   D. inlet

37. The fresh-air inlet plate at ⑬ is a part of the

    A. room ventilation
    B. air conditioning
    C. soil line
    D. vent line

38. The plumbing fitting at ⑯ is a

    A. trap   B. vent   C. meter   D. floor drain

39. The pipe at ⑲ is a

    A. hot water line
    B. cold water line
    C. soil line
    D. vent line

40. The purpose of the curb box at ⑳ is to permit

    A. checking the water flor
    B. checking the water pressure
    C. the water to be shut off
    D. determination of water purity

## KEY (CORRECT ANSWERS)

| | | | |
|---|---|---|---|
| 1. C | 11. C | 21. B | 31. C |
| 2. B | 12. C | 22. D | 32. A |
| 3. C | 13. B | 23. D | 33. D |
| 4. D | 14. B | 24. D | 34. B |
| 5. D | 15. C | 25. C | 35. C |
| 6. C | 16. D | 26. D | 36. C |
| 7. B | 17. C | 27. B | 37. D |
| 8. D | 18. D | 28. C | 38. A |
| 9. B | 19. D | 29. C | 39. C |
| 10. C | 20. D | 30. D | 40. C |

# TEST 2

DIRECTIONS: Each question or incomplete statement is followed by several suggested answers or completions. Select the one that BEST answers the question or completes the statement.

1. Maintenance workers are required to report defective equipment to their superiors even when the maintenance of the particular equipment is handled by another department. The PURPOSE of this rule is to

    A. keep employees alert
    B. reward employees who keep their eyes open
    C. pinpoint what department is falling down on its job
    D. have repairs made before serious trouble occurs

2. The MOST important reason for training employees is to

    A. satisfy their ego
    B. satisfy the unions
    C. improve the employees' ability to do a good job
    D. keep the supervisory personnel on their toes

3. The BEST first aid for an unconscious person lying on the ground is to

    A. sit him up
    B. cover his body with a blanket
    C. give him something to drink
    D. remove his outer clothing to keep him cool

4. The rules prohibit the use of the telephones for personal calls. The MOST important reason for this rule is that such personal calls

    A. cost the Authority money
    B. require additional telephone operators
    C. may tie up the telephone when needed for Authority business
    D. take the men away from their work

5. Of the following, the MAIN purpose of a safety training program is to

    A. fix the blame for accidents
    B. describe accidents which have occurred
    C. make the men aware of the basic causes of accidents
    D. maintain job progress under unsafe working conditions

6. Sharp edged tools should not be carried in a maintainer's pocket MAINLY because the

    A. tool's edge may become damaged
    B. tool is more readily lost
    C. tool may injure the maintainer
    D. maintainer may take the tool back to the locker room

Questions 7-13.

DIRECTIONS: Questions 7 through 13 refer to the sketches below. In answering these questions refer to the appropriate sketch.

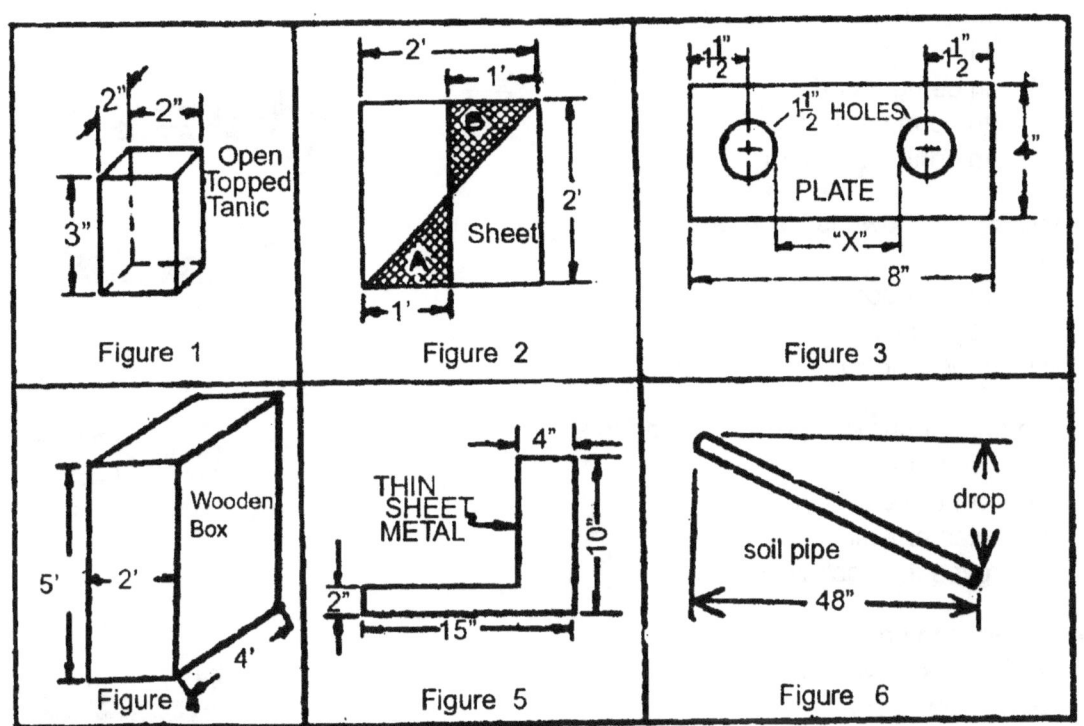

7. The MAXIMUM amount of water that the tank in Figure 1 can hold is 7.____
   A. 4 cu.in.    B. 6 cu.in.    C. 8 cu.in.    D. 12 cu.in.

8. The external surface area of sheet metal used to make the tank in Figure 1 is 8.____
   A. 12 sq.in.    B. 24 sq.in.    C. 28 sq.in.    D. 32 sq.in.

9. The MAXIMUM number of triangular pieces, equal in area to A or B in Figure 2, which can be cut from the full sheet is 9.____
   A. 4    B. 6    C. 8    D. 10

10. The distance "X" between the circular holes in Figure 3 is 10.____
    A. 2"    B. 3"    C. 3 1/2"    D. 5 1/2"

11. The MINIMUM amount of plywood needed to make the closed wood-en box in Figure 4 is 11.____
    A. 56.sq.ft.    B. 60 sq.ft.    C. 76 sq.ft.    D. 80 sq.ft.

12. The surface area of the sheet metal shape shown in Figure 5 is 12.____
    A. 42 sq.in.    B. 52 sq.in.    C. 62 sq.in.    D. 70 sq.in.

13. If the soil pipe in Figure 6 has a pitch of 1/2" per foot, the TOTAL drop in a horizontal run of 48 feet is 13.____
    A. 2 feet    B. 3 feet    C. 4 feet    D. 5 feet

Questions 14-24.

DIRECTIONS: In questions 14 through 24, the item referred to is shown to the right of the question.

14. The bolt shown should be used
    A. in foundations
    B. in cement curbs
    C. to connect rails
    D. to connect girders

14.____

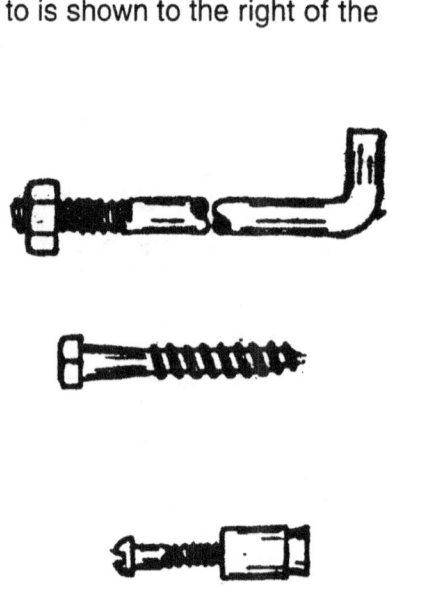

15. The screw shown is called a
    A. set screw
    B. anchor screw
    C. lag screw
    D. toggle screw

15.____

16. The anchor shown should be used in a
    A. wood post
    B. concrete wall
    C. plaster wall
    D. gypsum block wall

16.____

17. The wrench shown is called a(n)
    A. monkey wrench
    B. Allen wrench
    C. "L" wrench
    D. socket wrench

17.____

18. The anchor shown should be used in a
    A. concrete wall
    B. veneer wall
    C. plaster wall
    D. brick wall

18.____

19. The cutter shown should be used on
    A. pipes
    B. cables
    C. re-bars
    D. bolts

19.____

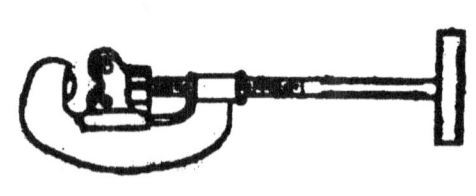

20. The saw shown is called a
    A. coping saw
    B. cross-cut saw
    C. hack saw
    D. back saw

20.____

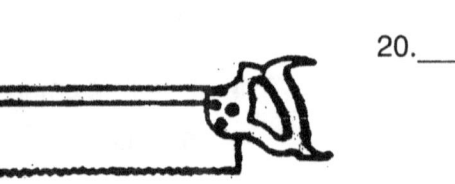

21. The tool shown is a
    A. "D" clamp
    B. "C" clamp
    C. pipe vise
    D. metal vise

21.____

64

22. The tool shown is a
    A. hawk
    B. trowel
    C. screed
    D. joiner

23. The tool shown is called a
    A. try square
    B. T-bevel
    C. miter box
    D. miter square

24. The tool shown should be used to
    A. make grooves in side walks
    B. turn lead bends
    C. make copper bends
    D. finish brick joints

25. All employees are required to give their names and badge numbers, without delay or argument, to any passenger who may request this information. The MAIN reason for this rule is that
    A. the subwsys are publicly owned
    B. essentially the passenger is the employer
    C. the passenger may be a policeman in plain clothes
    D. it makes for better public relations

26. The MAIN purpose of weep holes in cavity wall construction is to
    A. permit expansion
    B. help cure the concrete
    C. insulate the walls
    D. drain off moisture

27. The information in an accident report which may be MOST useful in decreasing the number of similar accidents is the
    A. number of people involved
    B. cause of the accident
    C. extent of the injuries sustained
    D. time the accident happened

28. The transit police must be notified first whenever an ambulance is needed. The MAIN reason for this rule is to
    A. prevent duplication of calls
    B. prevent ambulances from being sent to non-transit accidents
    C. allow the police to determine the need of an ambulance
    D. insure that the police are on hand

29. The MAIN purpose of giving employees instructions in first aid is to
    A. reduce the number of accidents
    B. save money on compensation causes
    C. eliminate the need for calling doctors
    D. enable them to provide emergency aid if needed

30. When steel is given two coats of paint, a different color is used for the second coat MAINLY to

A. insure that two coats were actually applied
B. insure full coverage by the second coat
C. prevent electrolysis
D. avoid painting in the field

Questions 31-40.

DIRECTIONS: Questions 31 through 40 deal with relationships between sets of figures. For each question, select that choice (A, or B, or C, or D) which has the SAME relationship to Figure 3 that Figure 2 has to Figure 1.

SAMPLE: Study Figures 1 and 2 in the SAMPLE. Notice that Figure 1 has been turned clockwise 1/4 of a turn to get Figure 2. Taking Figure 3 and turning it clockwise 1/4 of a turn, we get choice A, the correct answer.

## KEY (CORRECT ANSWERS)

| | | | |
|---|---|---|---|
| 1. D | 11. C | 21. B | 31. C |
| 2. C | 12. C | 22. B | 32. B |
| 3. B | 13. A | 23. C | 33. D |
| 4. C | 14. A | 24. A | 34. A |
| 5. C | 15. C | 25. D | 35. B |
| 6. C | 16. B | 26. D | 36. C |
| 7. D | 17. B | 27. B | 37. A |
| 8. C | 18. C | 28. A | 38. B |
| 9. C | 19. A | 29. D | 39. B |
| 10. C | 20. D | 30. B | 40. D |

# EXAMINATION SECTION
# TEST 1

DIRECTIONS: Each question or incomplete statement is followed by several suggested answers or completions. Select the one that BEST answers the question or completes the statement. *PRINT THE LETTER OF THE CORRECT ANSWER IN THE SPACE AT THE RIGHT.*

Questions 1-15.

DIRECTIONS: Questions 1 through 15 refer to the following tools. The numbers in the answers refer to the numbers beneath the tools.

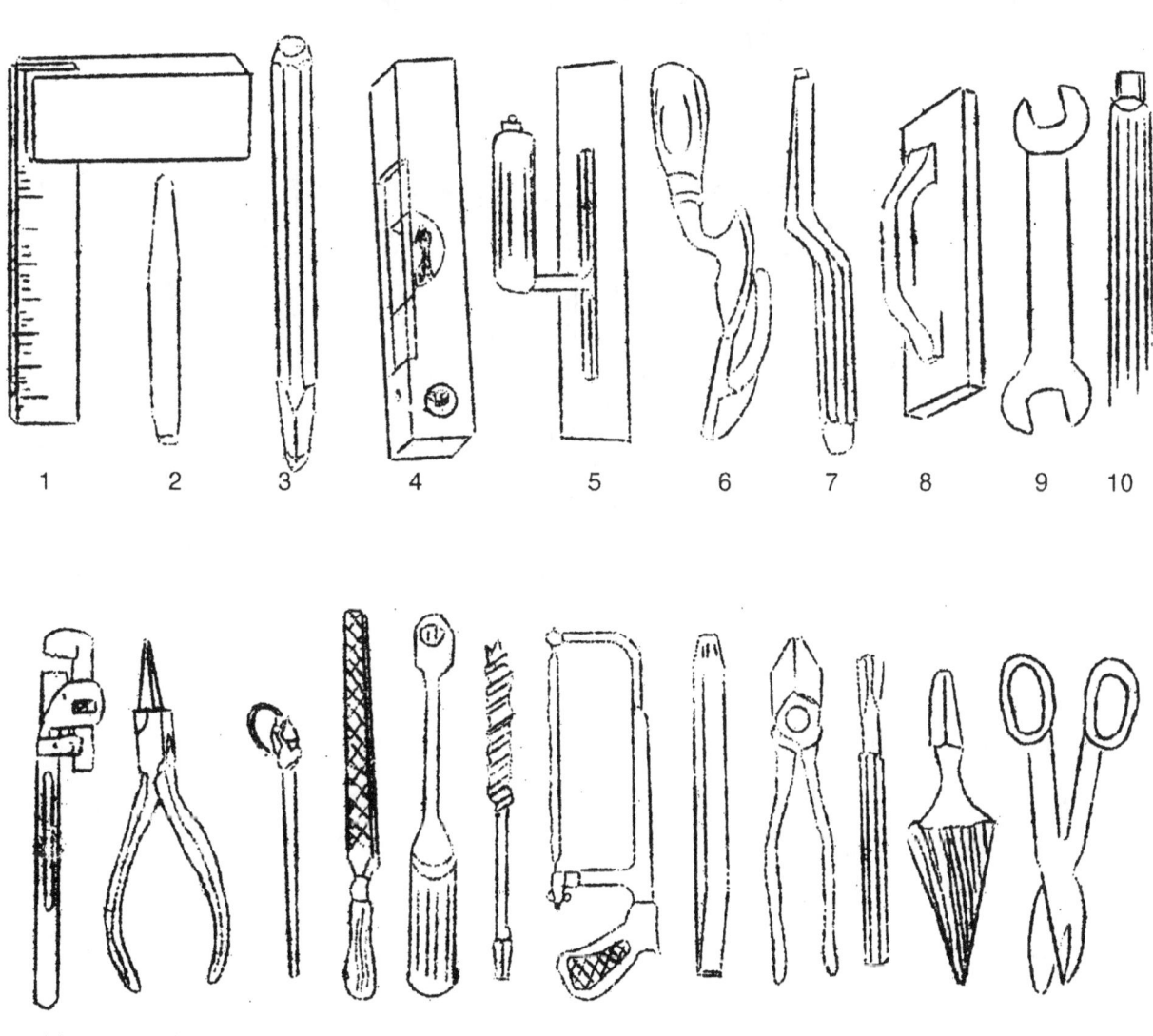

2 (#1)

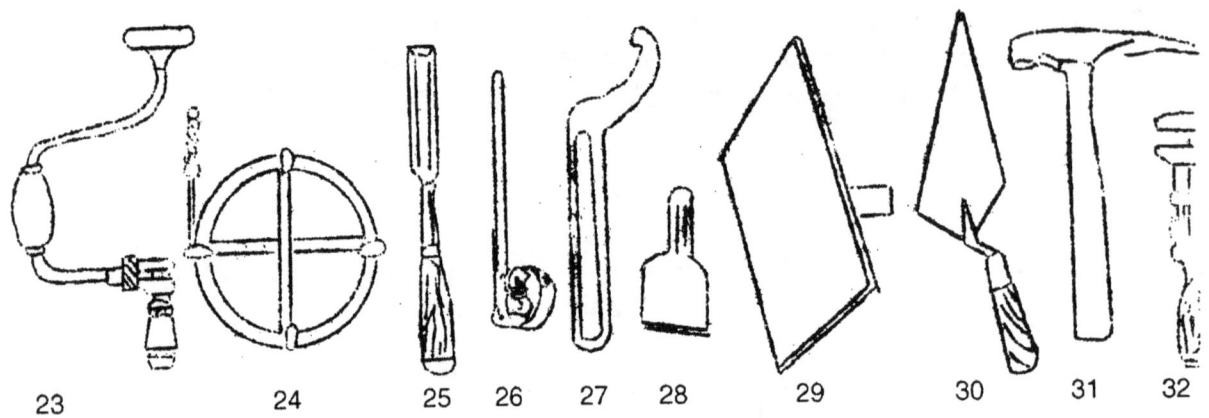

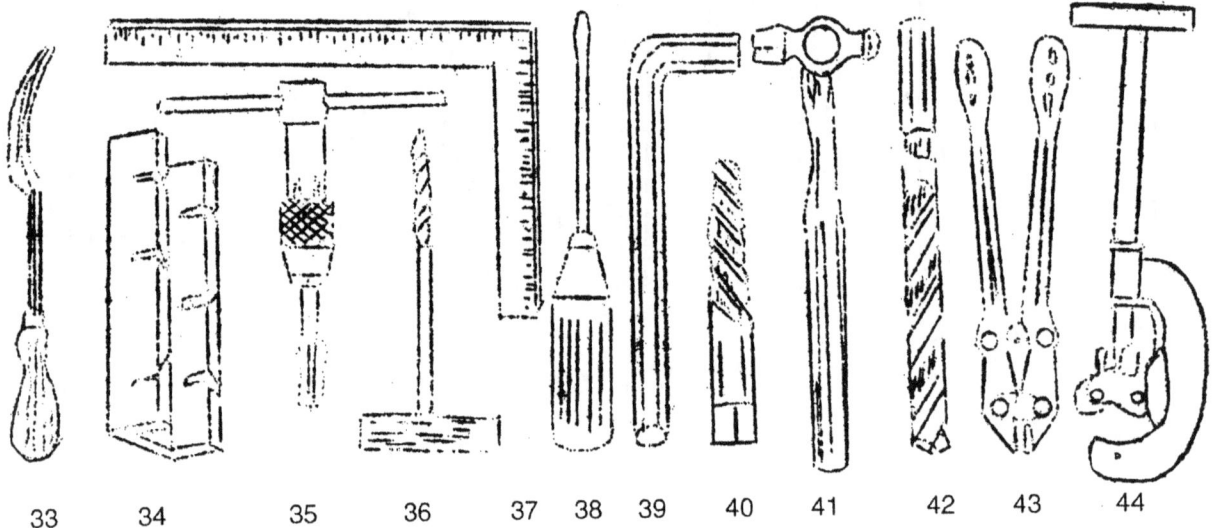

1. A *pipe reamer* is tool number
   A. 2        B. 10        C. 21        D. 24

2. A *mitre box* is tool number
   A. 1        B. 4         C. 25        D. 34

3. A *bolt cutter* is tool number
   A. 3        B. 25        C. 40        D. 43

4. The proper *drill bit* for wood is tool number
   A. 10       B. 16        C. 21        D. 40

5. A *ball peen* is tool number
   A. 20       B. 31        C. 33        D. 41

1.\_\_\_\_

2.\_\_\_\_

3.\_\_\_\_

4.\_\_\_\_

5.\_\_\_\_

6. A *hawk* is tool number  6._____
   A. 5   B. 28   C. 29   D. 30

7. *Snips* is tool number  7._____
   A. 12   B. 19   C. 22   D. 43

8. A *bull point* is tool number  8._____
   A. 3   B. 7   C. 10   D. 20

9. An *open-end wrench* is tool number  9._____
   A. 9   B. 11   C. 15   D. 27

10. A *drift pin* is tool number  10._____
    A. 2   B. 3   C. 10   D. D, 40

11. A *pipe cutter* is tool number  11._____
    A. 17   B. 18   C. 28   D. 44

12. A *trowel* is tool number  12._____
    A. 6   B. 8   C. 28   D. 30

13. A *square* is tool number  13._____
    A. 4   B. 29   C. 34   D. 37

14. A *float* is tool number  14._____
    A. 8   B. 28   C. 29   D. 30

15. A *snake* is tool number  15._____
    A. 13   B. 24   C. 26   D. 36

16. The volume of concrete in a strip of sidewalk 30 feet long by 4 feet wide by 3 inches thick is _____ cubic feet.  16._____
    A. 30   B. 120   C. 240   D. 360

17. The side support for steps or stairs is called a  17._____
    A. riser             B. stringer
    C. runner            D. ledger board

18. The machine which should be used to bend sheet metal is called a  18._____
    A. planer   B. brake   C. router   D. miller

19. The MAIN reason why a maintainer who expects to be absent from work on sick leave is required to telephone in at least one hour prior to reporting time is to  19._____
    A. permit a medical examination to be scheduled
    B. enable a substitute to be found
    C. enable a doctor to be sent to his home
    D. give payroll sufficient time to adjust his pay

20. Of the following, the BEST method of removing a slight coating of rust that has formed on small tools is to

    A. rub away the rust with a dry cloth
    B. dissolve the rust with a slight coat of vaseline
    C. scrape off the rust with a sharp knife
    D. rub the area with kerosene and fine steel wool

21. The sum of 3 1/6", 4 1/4", 3 5/8", and 5 7/16" is

    A. 15 9/16"    B. 16 1/8"    C. 16 3/8"    D. 16 3/4"

22. If a maintainer comes upon a blue light while walking along the track, he should know that this indicates the location of both an emergency power cutoff and a(n)

    A. emergency tool box        B. telephone
    C. signal box                D. first aid kit

23. It is NOT considered good practice to use a cold chisel whose head is badly beaten out of shape mainly because the chisel

    A. will be impossible to dress properly
    B. will cut unevenly
    C. may not fit the holder on the grinder
    D. may be unsafe to use

24. The MAIN reason why maintainers should make statements concerning accidents only to authorized employees of the authority is that this practice

    A. prevents lawsuits
    B. avoids conflicting testimony
    C. permits hiding of facts that may be embarrassing
    D. prevents unofficial statements from being accepted as official

25. Tools with exposed sharp edges should NOT be carried in a maintainer's pockets unless suitable sheaths are used MAINLY because the

    A. tools may break
    B. tools may get lost easily
    C. edges may become dull
    D. exposed edges may injure the maintainer

26. Safe practice dictates that, when using a portable electric drill, a maintainer should

    A. run it at slow speed
    B. ground the drill frame
    C. connect a lamp in series with the cord
    D. connect a lamp in parallel with the cord

27. Extending the handle of a wrench by using a piece of pipe to increase leverage when making up pipe is considered bad practice MAINLY because the

A. pipe threads may be stripped
B. pipe may be bent out of round
C. wrench may be damaged
D. pipe may slip off the wrench

28. If the head of a common hammer has become loose on the handle, of the following methods, it can BEST be tightened by

    A. driving the handle further into the head
    B. driving a nail alongside the existing wedge
    C. soaking the handle in water overnight
    D. replacing the existing wedge with a larger one

28.____

29. Tiles 12" x 12" are used to lay a floor having the dimensions 10'0" x 12'0". The MINIMUM number of tiles needed to completely cover the floor is

    A. 60           B. 96           C. 120          D. 144

29.____

30. The MOST important factor governing the strength of a concrete mix is the ratio of cement to

    A. gravel                       B. water
    C. sand                         D. sand and gravel combined

30.____

# KEY (CORRECT ANSWERS)

| | | | |
|---|---|---|---|
| 1. | C | 16. | A |
| 2. | D | 17. | B |
| 3. | D | 18. | B |
| 4. | B | 19. | B |
| 5. | D | 20. | D |
| 6. | C | 21. | C |
| 7. | C | 22. | B |
| 8. | A | 23. | D |
| 9. | A | 24. | D |
| 10. | A | 25. | D |
| 11. | D | 26. | B |
| 12. | D | 27. | C |
| 13. | D | 28. | D |
| 14. | A | 29. | C |
| 15. | B | 30. | B |

# TEST 2

DIRECTIONS: Each question or incomplete statement is followed by several suggested answers or completions. Select the one that BEST answers the question or completes the statement. *PRINT THE LETTER OF THE CORRECT ANSWER IN THE SPACE AT THE RIGHT.*

1. In order to permit the drainage of moisture, weep holes are placed in some types of walls.
   Such *weep holes* are USUALLY placed in _____ walls.

   A. veneered  B. solid brick
   C. combination  D. cavity

   1._____

2. In order to reduce damage in the event of a fire, most building codes require certain members to be fire cut. A *fire cut* is made in a

   A. rafter  B. stud  C. joist  D. column

   2._____

3. Chases should be used when erecting a building with brick walls.
   A *chase* is like a

   A. projection  B. parapet
   C. recess  D. belt course

   3._____

4. Some pieces of equipment have air valves which enable them to operate properly.
   An *air valve* is NORMALLY found on a

   A. sink  B. water closet
   C. radiator  D. vent stack

   4._____

5. Lintels are used to carry the weight of a wall above a window.
   A *lintel* is SIMILAR to a

   A. sill  B. truss  C. beam  D. column

   5._____

6. A bricklayer will make frequent use of bats when erecting veneered walls.
   A *bat* is a

   A. metal anchor  B. type of jointing tool
   C. cutting device  D. part of a brick

   6._____

7. It is usually necessary to caulk the windows when painting a building.
   This *caulking* operation is ESSENTIALLY one of

   A. cutting  B. smoothing  C. roughing  D. filling

   7._____

8. Structural steel members come in several different shapes. A steel *channel* has a cross-section shaped like a(n)

   A. H  B. I  C. U  D. Z

   8._____

9. Sheet metal workers frequently peen the rivets they use in fabricating ducts.
   To *peen* a rivet, you should _____ it.

   A. heat  B. flatten  C. cut  D. lengthen

   9._____

10. Skilled carpenters use a nail set to produce good work. A *nail set* should be used to

    A. measure nail size
    B. straighten nails
    C. sink nail heads into wood
    D. locate nails

11. When erecting structural steel, it is sometimes necessary for the iron workers to ream some of the bolt holes.
    To *ream* a hole is to _____ it.

    A. enlarge    B. straighten    C. locate    D. plug

12. Chuck keys are sometimes misplaced in a shop. A *chuck key* is closely associated with a

    A. combination lock        B. come-along
    C. drill                   D. hoist

13. A type of saw that should be found in the tool kit of a good carpenter is a coping saw.
    A *coping saw* should be used to cut

    A. BX cable                B. cast iron soil pipe
    C. 6" x 6" timber          D. thin wood

14. If a plumber was told that a trap is blocked, he should inspect a certain part of the plumbing system.
    A *trap* should NORMALLY be found in a

    A. hot water line          B. cold water line
    C. vent stack              D. soil line

15. A mallet may be used by a sheet metal worker to fabricate a drip pan.
    A *mallet* is a type of

    A. chisel                  B. screwdriver
    C. hammer                  D. pliers

16. One side of a wood form for a cement wall is 64 feet long by 8 feet high.
    If this form is to be made from 3/4" boards, 8 inches wide by 16 feet long, then the MINIMUM number of boards needed is

    A. 40    B. 48    C. 56    D. 64

17. Of the following, the MAIN reason for using a vibrator when placing concrete is to

    A. increase the air-entrained content
    B. prevent settling-out of the cement
    C. move the concrete into the forms
    D. eliminate air pockets

18. It is considered good practice to release the pressure from an air hose before uncoupling the hose connections MAINLY because this prevents

    A. damage to the air compressor
    B. damage to the hose
    C. compressed air from being wasted
    D. possible personal injury

19. If the allowable load on a wood scaffold is 30 pounds per square foot, then the MAXIMUM total load that should be permitted on a scaffold 4 feet wide by 18 feet long is _____ pounds.

   A. 540　　　B. 1680　　　C. 2160　　　D. 2720

20. The location where manila scaffold ropes are stored should be

   A. hot and dry
   B. hot and humid
   C. cool and dry
   D. cool and humid

21. A vertical wood framing member used in making a wall for a building is called a

   A. header　　　B. joist　　　C. beam　　　D. stud

22. The teeth of a hacksaw are usually set so as to make a cut wider than the saw blade. This is done MAINLY to _____ the blade.

   A. cool
   B. strengthen the teeth of
   C. prevent dulling
   D. permit easy movement of

23. Of the following, the MOST likely cause of a drill breaking while drilling into a steel plate is that the

   A. steel is too soft
   B. drill feed is excessive
   C. drill speed is too slow
   D. drill is too dull

24. Good practice dictates that a cold chisel should be kept free of oil or grease. The MAIN reason for this is to

   A. make the chisel cut better
   B. prevent splattering of oil when the chisel is struck
   C. eliminate a fire hazard when the chisel is sharpened
   D. prevent a hammer from glancing off the chisel head

25. If a pump can deliver 50 gallons of water per minute, then the time needed for this pump to empty an excavation containing 5800 gallons of water is _____ hr(s), _____ min.

   A. 2; 12　　　B. 1; 56　　　C. 1; 44　　　D. 1; 32

## KEY (CORRECT ANSWERS)

1. D
2. C
3. C
4. C
5. C

6. D
7. D
8. C
9. B
10. C

11. A
12. C
13. D
14. D
15. C

16. B
17. D
18. D
19. C
20. C

21. D
22. D
23. B
24. D
25. B

# TEST 3

DIRECTIONS: Each question or incomplete statement is followed by several suggested answers or completions. Select the one that BEST answers the question or completes the statement. *PRINT THE LETTER OF THE CORRECT ANSWER IN THE SPACE AT THE RIGHT.*

Questions 1-5.

DIRECTIONS: Questions 1 through 5 refer to commonly used materials, which are ordered by one of the quantity terms listed. Answer these questions by selecting the most commonly used unit of quantity for each given type of material.

1. 3/4" plywood

   A. feet
   C. sheets
   B. square feet
   D. pounds

   1._____

2. Builders' sand

   A. pounds
   C. cubic feet
   B. cubic yards
   D. barrels

   2._____

3. 5/8" steel cable

   A. pounds
   C. feet
   B. hundredweight
   D. lbs/sq.in.

   3._____

4. 3/16" steel rivets

   A. piece    B. pounds    C. dozen    D. thousand

   4._____

5. 4" cast iron pipe

   A. feet
   C. lengths
   B. pounds
   D. cubic feet

   5._____

6. The PROPER method of making an *eye* at the end of a wire rope is to use

   A. cleats    B. whippings    C. clips    D. nosings

   6._____

7. Reinforced concrete is concrete which has been strengthened by the addition of

   A. retarders
   C. rebars
   B. accelerators
   D. sodium chloride

   7._____

8. The MAIN reason for pitching steam pipes in a heating system is to

   A. make the repair of the system easier
   B. reduce friction in the pipes
   C. prevent the build-up of condensed steam
   D. make assembly of the system easier

   8._____

9. To change a quantity of cubic feet into an equivalent quantity of cubic yards, _____ the quantity by _____.

   A. multiply; 9
   C. multiply; 27
   B. divide; 9
   D. divide; 27

   9._____

10. The rules of the authority require that any request for an ambulance must be made only through the police.
    Of the following, the MOST likely reason for this requirement is that it

    A. permits the police to investigate first
    B. prevents more than one ambulance from being sent
    C. discourages unnecessary calls
    D. insures that the police are responsible

11. To obtain a measured degree of tightness on a nut, the wrench which should be used is a(n) _____ wrench.

    A. spanner     B. Stillson     C. torque     D. alligator

12. The gauge of sheet metal refers to a sheet's

    A. length          B. thickness
    C. area            D. width

13. A union is a plumbing fitting that is MOST commonly used to join

    A. a gate valve to an angle valve
    B. a gate valve to a threaded pipe
    C. two pieces of threaded pipe of the same diameter
    D. two pieces of threaded pipe of different diameters

14. A valve which permits water to flow in only one direction in a pipe is called a(n) _____ valve.

    A. check     B. globe     C. gate     D. angle

15. When sheet metal is riveted, a specified minimum distance must be provided between the edge of the sheet and the nearest rivet in order to prevent

    A. excessive stress concentrations on the rivet
    B. the rivet from being sheared off
    C. the rivet head from working loose
    D. tearing the sheet

## KEY (CORRECT ANSWERS)

| | | | |
|---|---|---|---|
| 1. | C | 6. | C |
| 2. | B | 7. | C |
| 3. | C | 8. | C |
| 4. | B | 9. | D |
| 5. | C | 10. | B |

11. C
12. B
13. C
14. A
15. D

---

# EXAMINATION SECTION
## TEST 1

DIRECTIONS: Each question or incomplete statement is followed by several suggested answers or completions. Select the one that BEST answers the question or completes the statement. *PRINT THE LETTER OF THE CORRECT ANSWER IN THE SPACE AT THE RIGHT.*

1. The seal of a trap is made of

    A. a bronze gate
    B. a bronze ball
    C. water
    D. air

    1.____

2. When a plumber is using a turnpin, he SHOULD be

    A. removing kinks from a lead bend
    B. cleaning a lead joint for wiping
    C. straightening out a piece of lead pipe
    D. flaring the end of a lead pipe

    2.____

3. A water meter measures and registers water consumption in

    A. gallons per minute
    B. cubic feet per hour
    C. quarts per second
    D. cubic feet

    3.____

4. The part that is connected to a ballcock that insures a full trap seal is the

    A. float ball
    B. upper liftrod
    C. hush tube
    D. refill tube

    4.____

5. PROPER protection against excessive pressure within a hot water storage tank is provided by installing a _____ valve.

    A. pressure relief
    B. check
    C. flow
    D. gate

    5.____

6. A one-sixteenth bend is EQUIVALENT to a fitting having an angle of _____ degrees.

    A. 22 1/2      B. 30      C. 45      D. 60

    6.____

7. A 3-inch standard weight water pipe and a 3-inch extra heavy water pipe have the SAME

    A. I.D.
    B. O.D.
    C. wall thickness
    D. weight per foot

    7.____

8. Of the following materials, the one that is NOT used in caulking a cast iron bell and spigot water pipe joint is

    A. asbestos rope
    B. oakum rope
    C. treated paper rope
    D. molded rings

    8.____

9. The reason a cast iron hub is hit before joining the hub with a spigot is to determine its

    A. soundness
    B. weight
    C. wall thickness
    D. material content

    9.____

10. The inside diameter of a 4" brass caulking ferrule is MOST NEARLY

    A. 3 7/8"  B. 4"  C. 4 1/8"  D. 4 1/4"

11. Cast brass floor flanges used for water closets should have a MINIMUM thickness of

    A. 1/2"  B. 3/8"  C. 1/4"  D. 1/8"

12. The trap of a water closet is located

    A. in the water closet
    B. in the lead bend
    C. under the water closet
    D. in the soil stack

13. Of the following, a PROPER reason why a plumber should install a check valve is to

    A. relieve pressure in the storage tank
    B. prevent a backflow of sewer gas
    C. allow a flow of water in one direction only
    D. reduce the volume of water in an appliance

14. The PURPOSE of an air chamber in a water line is to

    A. allow for expansion of water
    B. increase water pressure in the riser
    C. reduce water hammer in the system
    D. decrease velocity of the flow of water

15. As used by a plumber, a leader is a

    A. section of a soil stack
    B. vertical storm water pipe line
    C. part of a bath waste
    D. part of a croton

16. The bib-screw in a faucet retains the

    A. seat
    B. handle
    C. washer
    D. packing nut

17. When testing for leaks in gas lines, it is BEST to use

    A. water in the lines under pressure
    B. a lighted candle
    C. an aquastat
    D. soapy water

18. Drain lines receiving the discharge from chemistry laboratory sinks should be made of

    A. galvanized steel
    B. duriron or pyrex
    C. cast iron
    D. brass or copper

19. Of the following, the one that is BEST to use when testing for leaks in a new gas pipe installation is a

    A. geiger counter
    B. vacuum gauge
    C. mercury column
    D. water column

20. A plumber should know that installing a globe valve on a cold water line will cut down the _____ of the water.

    A. volume
    B. temperature
    C. viscosity
    D. resistance

21. Of the following tools, the one which is NOT used when working a wiped joint is the

    A. drift plug
    B. bending iron
    C. reamer
    D. turnpin

22. The amount of lead to be used to complete a caulked cast iron soil joint should NOT be less than _____ of the diameter of the pipe.

    A. 10 ounces for each inch
    B. 12 ounces for each inch
    C. 14 ounces for each inch
    D. one full medium-sized ladle regardless

23. A shave hook is recommended by its manufacturer for

    A. evening the edges of lead
    B. brightening oxidized copper
    C. removing burrs from non-ferrous pipe
    D. removing oxidation from lead

24. The MAIN purpose of a house trap is to

    A. provide the house drain with a cleanout
    B. prevent gases from the public sewer from entering the house plumbing system
    C. *trap* articles of value that are lost
    D. eliminate the necessity for traps under all other fixtures

25. A corporation cock or stop is a

    A. self-closing faucet
    B. shut-off valve for a lavoratory
    C. frost-proof type of hydrant
    D. shut-off valve for a water service

26. A 45-degree offset included in a house drain should contain ONLY

    A. one 1/4 bend and one 1/16 bend
    B. one 1/4 bend and one 1/8 bend
    C. two 1/8 bends
    D. two 1/4 bends

27. A plumber prevents siphonage in a fixture trap if he

    A. vents properly
    B. installs a relief valve
    C. installs the correct number of check valves
    D. provides adequate pitch on the water lines

28. A 28 ft. long pipe line, stalled with a pitch of 1/4 inch per foot, has a TOTAL fall of _____ inches.

   A. 3 1/4    B. 7    C. 10 1/2    D. 14

29. The length of a pipe measuring 37.875 inches, end-to-end, is EQUAL to 3 ft. + _____ inches.

   A. 0 7/8    B. 1 1/4    C. 1 5/8    D. 1 7/8

30. A waste stack may receive the discharge from _____ water closet(s).

   A. no
   B. only one
   C. two
   D. three or more

31. Capillary action is used in the CORRECT joining of _____ joints.

   A. bell and spigot
   B. screw-pipe
   C. copper-tube sweat
   D. lead-wiped

32. The TOTAL length of four pieces of I 1/2" galvanized steel pipe whose lengths are 7 ft. + 3 1/2 inches, 4 ft. + 2 1/4 inches, 6 ft. +7 inches, and 8 ft. + 5 1/8 inches, is _____ ft. + _____ inches.

   A. 26; 5 7/8
   B. 25; 6 7/8
   C. 25; 4 1/4
   D. 25; 3 3/8

33. To a plumber, the letters I.P.S. mean

   A. internal pipe size
   B. iron pipe size
   C. interior pressure standards
   D. international pipe standard.

34. Of the following, the tool that SHOULD be used on polished pipe surface is the

   A. Stillson wrench
   B. strap wrench
   C. chain tongs
   D. crescent wrench

35. In plumbing, the abbreviation X.H.C.I. is associated with

   A. water heaters
   B. chemical waste lines
   C. air lines
   D. house drains

36. A yarning iron SHOULD be used in

   A. tinning copper fittings
   B. making lead safes
   C. making bell and spigot joints
   D. drying a water-filled trench

37. If a 45-degree offset is 12 inches in length, the length of its diagonal or travel is _____ inches.

   A. 17    B. 18    C. 19    D. 20

38. *Plumbers Soil* is GENERALLY used by plumbers as an aid in  38.____

    A. wiping lead joints
    B. making up flange joints
    C. backfilling a trench
    D. threading steel pipes

39. Of the following types of saws, the one that SHOULD be used for cutting lead pipe is the  39.____
    _____ saw.

    A. cross-cut
    B. rip
    C. hack
    D. dove-tail

40. Of the following fixtures, the one that plumbers USUALLY call the *unit fixture* is the  40.____

    A. water closet
    B. slop sink
    C. lavatory
    D. bathtub

# KEY (CORRECT ANSWERS)

| | | | |
|---|---|---|---|
| 1. C | 11. D | 21. C | 31. C |
| 2. D | 12. A | 22. B | 32. A |
| 3. D | 13. C | 23. D | 33. B |
| 4. D | 14. C | 24. B | 34. B |
| 5. A | 15. B | 25. D | 35. D |
| 6. A | 16. C | 26. C | 36. C |
| 7. B | 17. D | 27. A | 37. A |
| 8. B | 18. B | 28. B | 38. A |
| 9. A | 19. C | 29. D | 39. A |
| 10. D | 20. A | 30. A | 40. C |

# TEST 2

DIRECTIONS: Each question or incomplete statement is followed by several suggested answers or completions. Select the one that BEST answers the question or completes the statement. *PRINT THE LETTER OF THE CORRECT ANSWER IN THE SPACE AT THE RIGHT.*

1. The vertical distance between the crown weir and the dip of a trap is called the    1.____
   - A. jumpover
   - B. air gap
   - C. seal depth
   - D. diameter of the trap

2. Of the following, the composition of general purpose *wiping solder* is _____ tin and _____ lead.    2.____
   - A. 70%; 30%
   - B. 60%; 40%
   - C. 50%; 50%
   - D. 35%; 65%

3. Of the following wrenches, the one which should be used on screwed valves and fittings having hexagonal connections is the _____ wrench.    3.____
   - A. pipe
   - B. monkey
   - C. chuck
   - D. strap

4. A cast iron coupling that has one end threaded for screw pipe and the other end hubbed to receive the spigot end of a pipe is known as a(n)    4.____
   - A. sisson fitting
   - B. tucker fitting
   - C. union
   - D. F & W fitting

5. The size of a fresh-air inlet is based on the size of the associated    5.____
   - A. house drain
   - B. public sewer
   - C. house sewer
   - D. soil stack

6. The tool that holds the dies when pipe is being threaded is called a    6.____
   - A. yoke
   - B. vise
   - C. stock
   - D. swedge

7. A gallon of water weighs MOST NEARLY _____ lbs.    7.____
   - A. 6.25
   - B. 7.5
   - C. 8.33
   - D. 14.7

8. A *solder nipple* is MAINLY used in plumbing work to    8.____
   - A. maintain an even flow of solder
   - B. connect the handle of a soldering iron to the *copper*
   - C. make up a joint between lead pipe and brass pipe
   - D. clean clogged pipes

9. Where steel hangers are used to support copper pipe, the pipe should be insulated from the hangers to prevent    9.____
   - A. water hammer
   - B. vibration
   - C. cooling
   - D. electrolysis

10. Copper tubing having the GREATEST wall thickness is known as _____ copper tubing.    10.____
    - A. D.W.V. type
    - B. type M
    - C. type L
    - D. type K

11. Of the following methods, the BEST one to use in making up a pipe joint between lead pipe and copper pipe is      11.____

    A. brazing            B. soldering
    C. burning            D. wiping

12. To *break in* or condition a new asbestos joint runner, the runner SHOULD be soaked in      12.____

    A. alcohol    B. rosin    C. oil    D. water

13. The weight of a 4 ft. x 4 ft. shower pan made of 6-pound lead is MOST NEARLY _____ pounds.      13.____

    A. 96    B. 75    C. 69    D. 29.25

14. The approved method of making a branch connection to an existing horizontal cast iron wasteline is by using a      14.____

    A. sisson fitting         B. kaeffer fitting
    C. saddle                 D. three-piece connection

15. A *hydropneumatic* tank in a plumbing system is MAINLY used to      15.____

    A. pump storm water to the sewer
    B. provide potable water under pressure
    C. supply compressed air to equipment
    D. filter water for a swimming pool.

16. Syphon action through the fill pipe in a flush tank is prevented by installing a      16.____

    A. stop and waste valve    B. vacuum breaker
    C. flushometer             D. back-water valve

17. Sperm candle or tallon is applied to clean lead work in order to PREVENT      17.____

    A. pitting       B. oxidation
    C. tinning       D. melting

18. Joints for cast iron bell and spigot soil pipe SHOULD be made with      18.____

    A. wiped solder
    B. packed oakum and molten lead
    C. oakum and asphaltic compound
    D. oakum and cement mortar

19. A tee whose branch is larger than the run is CORRECTLY referred to as a _____ tee.      19.____

    A. bullhead    B. lateral    C. street    D. reducing

20. A house drain which is buried in earth SHOULD be made of      20.____

    A. galvanized wrought iron    B. galvanized steel
    C. transite                   D. uncoated cast iron

21. A compression type fitting is MOST frequently used with      21.____

    A. copper tubing    B. steel pipe
    C. transite         D. cast iron pipe

22. Safety goggles should be worn when cutting

    A. galvanized pipe  B. oakum
    C. cast iron  D. sheet lead

23. A plumber should NOT plunge a wet ladle into a pot of molten caulking lead because it

    A. contaminates the lead  B. may crack the pot
    C. may crack the ladle  D. makes the lead spatter

24. A plumber's helper who is careless is one who is

    A. negligent  B. untrained
    C. neat  D. methodical

25. A CORRECTLY installed gasket provides a seal in a

    A. flange union  B. ground joint union
    C. roof flange  D. left-right coupling

26. A plumber installing a battery of sinks in the kitchen of a school cafeteria should also include in the waste line a(n)

    A. chlorinator  B. anti-syphon loop
    C. grease trap  D. check valve

27. If a faucet continues to drip despite the new washer a helper has installed, he SHOULD then

    A. reface or replace the seat
    B. install a washer made of different material
    C. replace the entire faucet
    D. replace the bib-screw

28. Of the following tools, the one used to fasten faucets to lavatories is called a(n)

    A. pair of pump pliers  B. spud wrench
    C. open-end wrench  D. basin wrench

29. A cast iron floor flange SHOULD be used when installing a

    A. water closet  B. bathtub
    C. kitchen sink  D. drinking fountain

30. A plumber's rasp is a tool recommended by its manufacturer for use on

    A. cast iron  B. brass
    C. lead  D. black steel

31. Of the following, the pipe size NOT common to the plumbing trade is _____ inch.

    A. 2  B. 2 1/2  C. 3  D. 3 1/2

32. Once a flushometer valve is in operation, it is made to close automatically by the

    A. return of the lever handle to the neutral position
    B. action of a flat helical spring above the diaphragm
    C. water pressure on the inlet side of the valve
    D. elasticity of a stainless steel diaphragm

Questions 33-36.

DIRECTIONS: Questions 33 through 36, inclusive, are to be answered by referring to the following sketch of a piping arrangement.

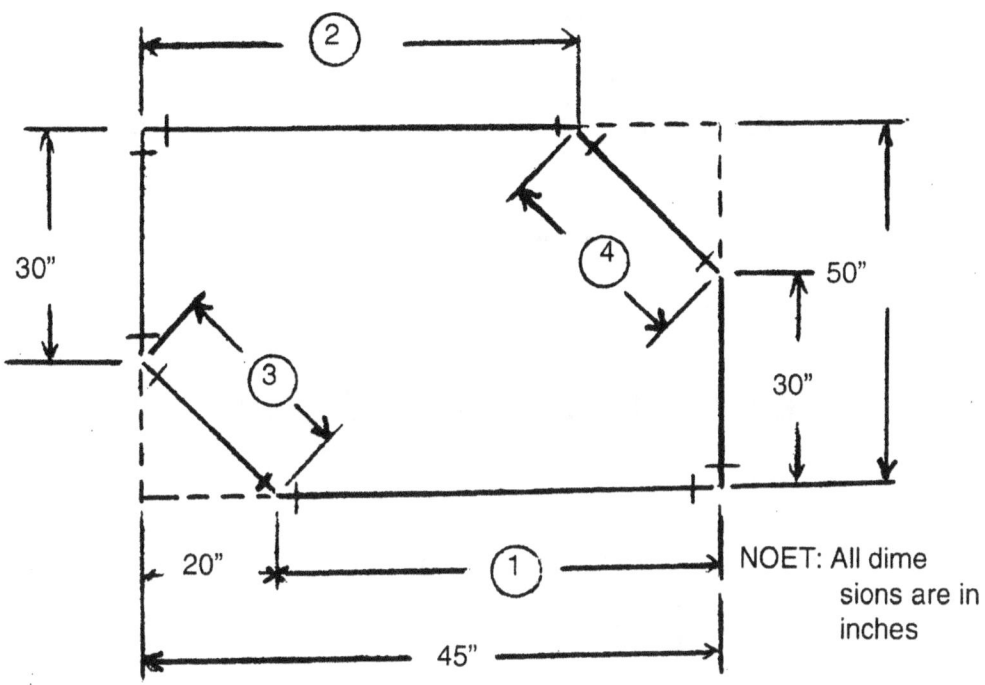

33. The center-to-center pipe measurement of *1* is MOST NEARLY equal to _____ inches.   33._____
    A. 20         B. 25         C. 30         D. 65

34. The center-to-center pipe measurement of *2* is MOST NEARLY equal to _____ inches.   34._____
    A. 20         B. 25         C. 30         D. 45

35. The center-to-center pipe measurement of *3* is MOST NEARLY equal to _____ inches.   35._____
    A. 30 1/2     B. 28 7/8     C. 28 1/4     D. 27 3/4

36. The center-to-center pipe measurement of *4* is MOST NEARLY equal to _____ inches.   36._____
    A. 23 1/2     B. 28 1/4     C. 29         D. 31 1/4

37. An outside caulking iron is a tool recommended by its manufacturer for use on   37._____
    A. steel pipe         B. cast iron
    C. lead pipe          D. brass pipe

38. A swimming pool is 25 feet wide by 75 feet long and has an average depth of 5 feet. The capacity when filled to the overflow is _____ gallons.   38._____
    A. 9,375      B. 65,625     C. 69,005     D. 70,312

39. A tap borer SHOULD be used by a plumber when 39.____
    A. cutting internal threads
    B. preparing copper joints for sweating
    C. joining cast iron to screw pipe
    D. preparing soil lead pipe for a solder nipple

40. A hydrostatic test on a plumbing system SHOULD be done by using 40.____
    A. water    B. smoke    C. air    D. kerosene

---

# KEY (CORRECT ANSWERS)

| | | | |
|---|---|---|---|
| 1. C | 11. D | 21. A | 31. D |
| 2. D | 12. C | 22. C | 32. C |
| 3. B | 13. A | 23. D | 33. B |
| 4. B | 14. D | 24. A | 34. B |
| 5. A | 15. B | 25. A | 35. C |
| 6. C | 16. B | 26. C | 36. B |
| 7. C | 17. B | 27. A | 37. B |
| 8. C | 18. B | 28. D | 38. D |
| 9. D | 19. A | 29. A | 39. D |
| 10. D | 20. D | 30. C | 40. A |

# BASIC PLUMBING

## TABLE OF CONTENTS

| | Page |
|---|---|
| PLANNING | 1 |
| ROUGHING-IN | 3 |
| WATER-SUPPLY PIPING | 4 |
|     Materials | 4 |
|     Size | 4 |
| DRAINAGE PIPING | 4 |
|     Materials | 5 |
|     Size and Slope | 6 |
|     Traps and Venting | 6 |
|     Floor Drains | 8 |
| PIPE FITTINGS AND CLEANOUTS | 9 |
|     Fittings | 9 |
|     Cleanouts | 10 |
| FIXTURES | 11 |
| WATER HEATERS | 13 |
| PROTECTING WATER PIPES FROM FREEZING | 14 |
| CONDENSATION | 15 |
| SERVICE BUILDING PLUMBING | 15 |
|     Water-Supply Piping | 15 |
|     Drainage Piping | 16 |

# BASIC PLUMBING

Careful planning and proper installation are essential for a safe and adequate plumbing system in the home or other farmstead buildings.

Installation of plumbing requires special knowledge and tools and should be done by, or under the guidance of, an experienced person. It must be done in accordance with applicable State, county, or local plumbing codes. Code requirements take precedence over recommendations given in this bulletin.

Planning the plumbing system should be done by the family, who know most about their own living habits and needs. A knowledge of the kinds of piping, fixtures, and other equipment required and available will aid in planning. Also, advice should be obtained from qualified persons.

## PLANNING

In planning a plumbing system, consider your future needs as well as your present. It costs less to install a few extra tees with plugs for future connections than it does to cut into a plumbing system to make connections later on.

Adding or remodeling plumbing in existing buildings involves the additional expense and labor of opening up walls or floors. It may be more economical to run piping along the exposed face of a wall or floor and then box it in for appearance.

In the home, there are at least three areas where water is needed the kitchen, the bathroom, and the laundry. Around the farmstead, water is needed in the dairy barn and milkhouse. in other buildings where stock are kept or watered, in the shop, and in the yard or family garden. The location of appliances, fixtures, and faucets in each of these areas must be planned in advance.

Planning a plumbing system also includes providing for proper drainage of wastes. Improper handling of wastes can lead to contamination of the water supply and consequent spread of diseases. Poor planning or workmanship can also mean hours of unpleasant work in repairing or clearing clogged drains.

Plumbing costs can often be kept down by good planning in locating fixtures. Fixtures located back to back on opposite sides of a wall, as shown in figure 1 on page 2, save on piping. Locating all bathroom fixtures on one wall, as shown in the illustration, also saves piping. In the arrangement shown in figure 1, one vent stack serves all fixtures.

Figure 2, on page 2, shows a vertical arrangement of fixtures to reduce the amount of piping needed in multi-storied houses. Locating fixtures in a continuous line, as shown in figures 3 and 4, saves piping in single-story houses.

A water heater should be located as close as practical to the fixture where hot water will be used most frequently. Long runs of hot water pipe result in unnecessary use of water and heat.

### Precautions

Every precaution must be taken to insure a safe water supply and otherwise protect the health of the family. When installing plumbing, be sure that

- There are no leaks in the drainage system through which sewage or sewer gases can escape.

- There are no cross connections between the water-supply system and any other piping carrying water or other materials.

- All fixtures are designed and installed so that there can be no back siphonage from the fixture into the water-supply system. This precaution also applies to fixtures, such as water bowls, installed in service buildings for use by animals.

2

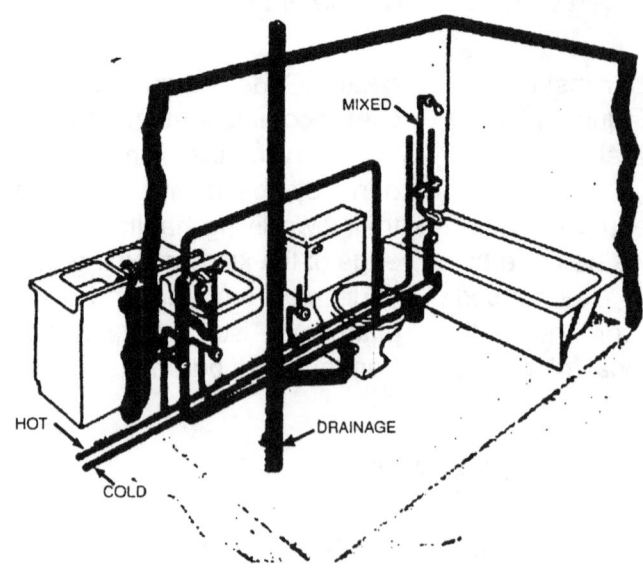

Figure 1 – Plumbing fixtures located back to back on opposite sides of a wall.

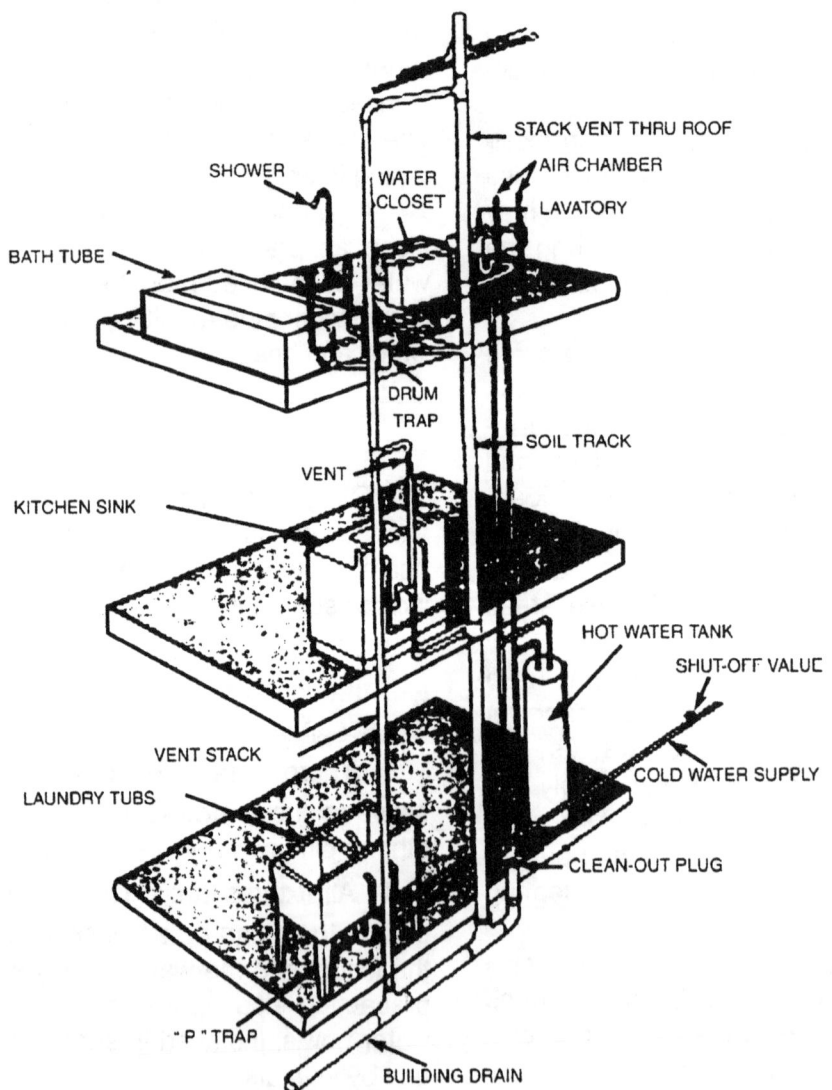

Figure 2 - Plumbing arrangement in a two-story house with basement.

# 3
# ROUGHING-IN

The term "roughing-in" refers to placing the piping that will be concealed in the walls or under the floors of a building during construction or remodeling. The fixtures are normally connected to this piping after construction work is completed. Future fixtures may also be provided for in this manner. Building drains may be laid under concrete floors before the superstructure framing is started.

Roughing-in includes installation and testing of the water-supply and drainage piping and the fixture supports. The location and height of sinks, lavatories, and other fixtures must be precisely indicated on the

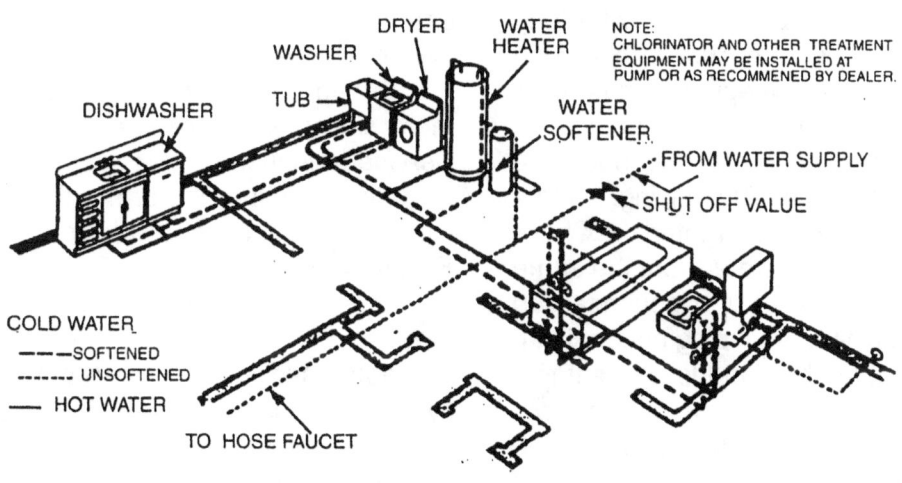

Figure 3 - A fixture and water-supply-piping layout for a one-story house.

building plans to insure correct installation of the piping and supports. For sinks a height of 36 inches and for lavatories a height of 33 to 35 inches, measured from the floor to the top of the rim, should suit most adults. Some families may find it more convenient to have the fixtures slightly higher or lower.

After the roughed-in work is completed, and before it is concealed, the plumbing system should be tested for leaks. Local plumbing codes usually include a standard testing procedure. Where no code is in effect, the drainage and water-supply systems may be tested as follows:

*Drainage system*—Tightly plug all openings, except the highest one. Fill the system with water, and let the water stand for about 15 minutes. Then check the entire system for leaks.

The system can be checked by sections. If done that way, test each section under a head (depth, measured vertically) of water of at least 10 feet to be sure that each section and joint will withstand at least that much pressure.

*Water-supply system*—This system can be tested in the same way as the drainage system, but only potable (drinkable) water should be used, and it should be under pressure at least equal to the working pressure of the system, but not less than 60 pounds per square inch. A pump and pressure gage will be needed to make the test.

# 4
# WATER-SUPPLY PIPING

## Materials

Galvanized pipe or copper tubing is normally used for water-supply, or distribution piping. However, these two materials should not be joined directly to each other (see p. 12).

Copper tubing may cost a little more than galvanized pipe, but it is easier to install and has a smoother inside surface.

Both hard-drawn (rigid) and soft-drawn (flexible) copper tubing are available. The soft-drawn tubing can be installed with long sweeping bends. Less pressure is lost when water runs through sweeping bends than when it makes abrupt changes in direction.

Characteristics of the water should be considered when selecting piping. Some waters corrode some piping materials. Check with neighbors who use water from the same water-bearing stratum; their experience can guide you in selecting the piping material. Or, have a chemical analysis made of a sample of the water. Your State college or university may be equipped to make an analysis. If not, it can direct you to a private laboratory. Firms in the water treatment equipment business make analyses for prospective customers.

## Size

Water-distribution piping should be as short and as straight as possible. The longer the pipe and the smaller its diameter, the greater the loss of pressure. Some pressurew is lost whenever water passes around bends and through elbows and other fittings.

To improve service by providing higher residual pressures, quieter operation, and reduced water hammer, the following water-velocity limits or specific pipe sizes are recommended:

*Service mains*

Buried lines to buildings: 1¼ inch minimum size pipe; 4 feet per second velocity.

*Service branches*

Lines serving one or more fixture supply lines: 6 feet per second velocity.

*Fixture supply lines*

Lines serving individual fixtures, as follows:

Automatic washer, hose bibbs, and wall hydrants: ¾-inch minimum pipe size.

Bathtub, dishwasher, kitchen sink, laundry trays, and shower stall: ½-inch minimum pipe size.

Lavatory and water closet: Check local plumbing code for specific requirements.

# DRAINAGE PIPING

The building drainage system includes all piping that carries sewage or other liquid waste to the building sewer, which, in turn, carries it to the disposal facility. Since the escape of sewage or sewer gases can be a serious health hazard, this system must be as carefully designed and installed as the water-distribution system.

A house or building drainage system generally includes these basic parts:

*Fixture drain*—The piping through which a fixture drains. Each fixture must be trapped and vented.

*Fixture branch*—A pipe connecting several fixture drains.

*Soil stack*—The vertical soil pipe into which the water closet or other fixture having a similar function drains, with or without the discharge from other fixtures. It connects to the building drain and is vented up through the roof to the outside air. The vent portion is called the stack vent.

*Building drain*—The main horizontal drain that receives the discharge from soil, waste, or other drainage pipes inside the building and carries it outside the building to the building sewer, which carries it to the disposal facility.

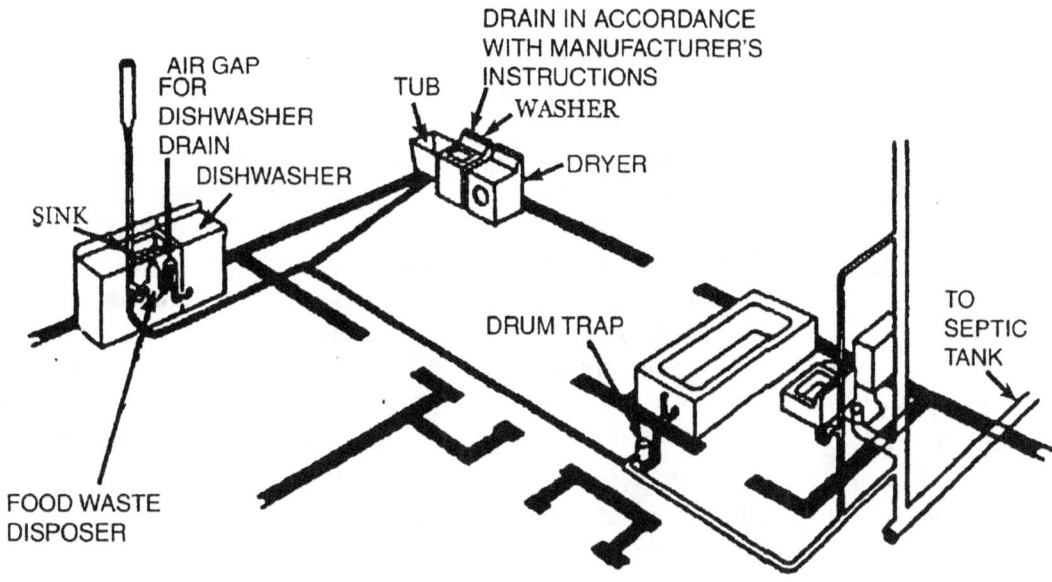

Figure 4 - Drainage system layout for the arrangement in figure 3.

## Plastic Piping

Carefully selected and properly installed plastic pipe offers several advantages over conventional piping materials such as galvanized steel and copper pipe or tube. There are no perfect plumbing materials and all must be installed with knowledge of their physical properties and limitations.

Today's plastic pipe and fittings are often the most economical and are nearly immune to the attack of aggressive waters. At this time PE (polyethylene) pipe is used most commonly for underground service. Since it is furnished in long coils, it requires a minimum of fittings for long piping runs. For short runs, the friction loss in the insert fittings is a disadvantage. PVC (polyvinyl-chloride) pipe is available in nearly twice the pressure rating for the same cost as PE. PVC pipe is most often assembled with solvent-welded fittings. Heavy-wall PVC Schedule 80 pipe may be threaded. CPVC (chlorinated-polyvinyl-chloride) pipe is available for hot water service.

ABS (acrilonitrile-butadienestyrene) pipe was once primarily used in potable water distribution in a size known as SWP (solvent-welded pipe). Today ABS is used in DWV (drainage-waste-vent) systems. PVC is also used in DWV systems.

To be sure of getting quality plastic pipe and fittings, make sure that the material is marked with the manufacturer's name or trademark, pipe size, the plastic material type or class code, pressure rating, standard to which the pipe is manufactured (usually an ASTM standard), and the seal of approval of an accredited testing laboratory (usually N.S.F. the National Sanitation Foundation).

### Materials

Drainage piping may be made of cast iron, galvanized wrought iron or steel, copper, brass, or plastic. Cast iron is commonly used for building drains that are buried under concrete floors or underground. Steel pipe should not be laid under-ground or under concrete.

## Size and Slope

Wastes normally flow through the drainage system by gravity. (Sometimes wastes flow by gravity to a sump, then are lifted by a pump.) The drainage piping must be of the proper size and slope to insure good flow.

Local plumbing codes should be checked for the sizes of drain pipe required. Minimum sizes recommended are:

|  | Minimum size in inches |
|---|---|
| *Piping for-* |  |
| Fixture drains: |  |
|   Bathtub, dishwasher, kitchen sink, and laundry trays | 1½ |
|   Lavatory | 1¼ |
|   Floor drain and shower stall | 2 |
|   Water closet | 3 |
| Fixture branch | 1½ |
| Soil stack | 3 |
| Building drain: |  |
|   Beyond soil stack connection | 3 |
|   Above soil stack connection | ([1]) |

[1] Not less than connecting branch.

Horizontal drainpipes—pipes that slope less than 45° from the horizontal—3 inches or less in diameter should slope at least one-fourth of an inch per foot. Larger pipes should slope not less than one-eighth of an men per foot.

## Traps and Venting

Gases develop in sewers and septic tanks and flow back through the drainage piping system. To prevent these gases from backing up through open fixture drains or over-flows and escaping into the house, a trap is required at each fixture (figs. 5 and 6). The trap should be the same size as the drainpipe and as close as possible to the fixture outlet. The water seal in the trap should be at least 2 inches, but not more than 4 inches. Water closets usually have built-in traps and no additional one is required. Never double-trap a fixture.

## Grease Traps

A grease trap is different from a fixture trap and serves an entirely different purpose. It is designed to prevent greases and fats from entering a sewerage system. It should be used only where large amounts of grease may be discharged into the waste disposal system for example, in a restaurant or boarding house. It is not needed in the average dwelling.

If used, a grease trap should not receive the discharge from a food waste disposer. Grease accumulations must be removed from the trap at frequent intervals.

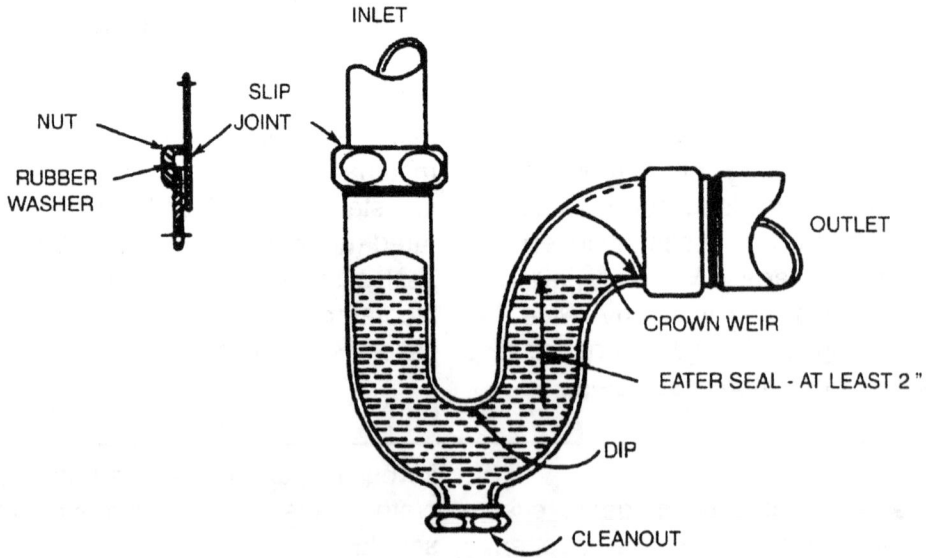

Figure 5 - P trap assembly.

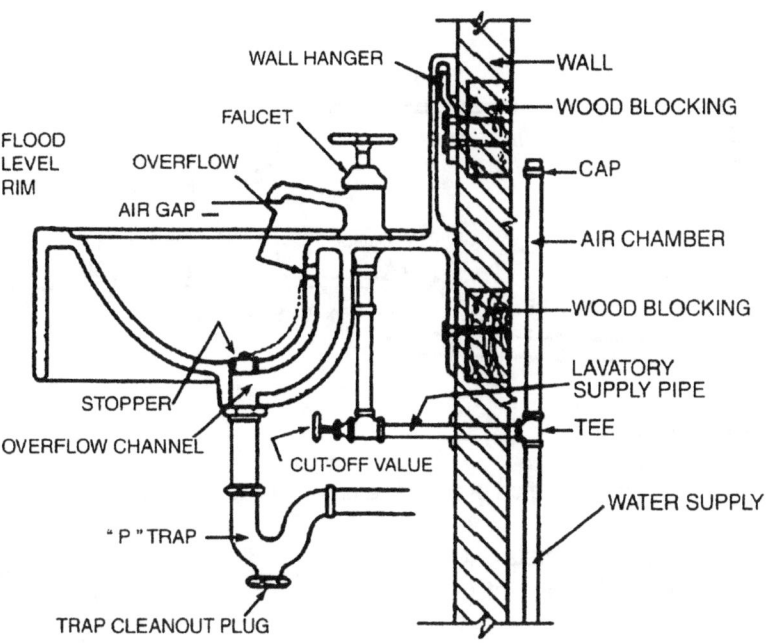

Figure 6 - Lavatory, showing water-supply and drainage piping. Note air gap at faucet and air chamber. An air chamber prevents water hammer.

Drum traps (see fig. 7) are commonly used in bathtub drain lines. A trap should be 3 or 4 inches in diameter, and the bottom or top should be removable to permit cleaning of the trap and drainpipe.

Sewer gases that are confined can develop pressure and bubble through the water seal in fixture traps. Therefore, at least one vent must be provided through which these gases can escape to the outside air and thus prevent any build up of pressure or vacuum on the trap seal.

The soil stack should always be vented to the outside, above the roof and undiminished in size. Additional vents directly to the outside may be needed or required for individual fixtures. Plumbing codes specify the venting required. Where there is no code, the recommendations given herein may be followed.

A vent pipe (or stack, as the vertical portion is called) should extend far enough above the roof to prevent it from being blocked by snow, but at least 6 inches. The opening in the roof through which the pipe passes must be flashed (tightly sealed) to make it watertight (fig. 8).

In very cold climates, the part of a vent above the roof should be at least 3 inches in diameter to prevent frost closure in cold weather. Where individual vents are used for fixtures, 1½-inch pipe is recommended. Vent increasers (see fig. 8) may be used to increase the diameter of the vent stacks above the roof.

Each fixture drain must be vented to prevent the siphoning of the water from the fixture trap. Figures 1, 2, 4, and 7 show the methods of venting fixture drains. Vent piping for each fixture should be installed between the trap and the sewerline, and should be the same size as the drain piping. If connected to the soil stack, the vent piping should be connected above the highest fixture drain. Otherwise, it should extend separately to above the roof. The distance from the fixture trap to the vent is governed by the size of the fixture drain. Maximum distances recommended are:

8

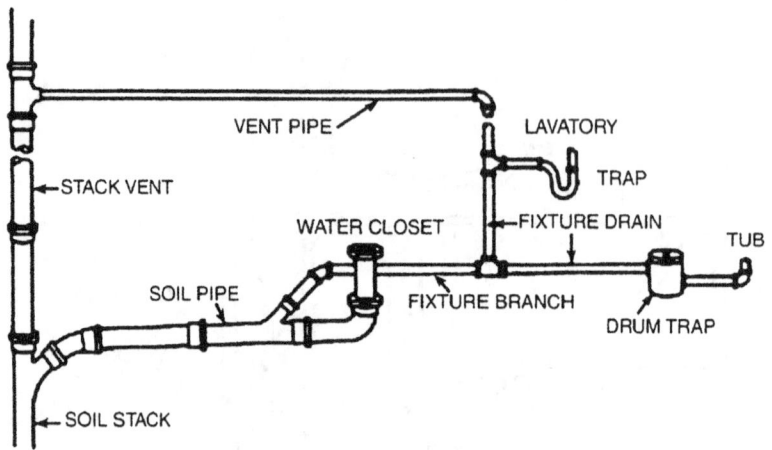

Figure 7 - Method of venting a group of bathroom fixtures.

| Size of fixture drain (inches) | Maximum distance from trap to vent (feet) |
| --- | --- |
| 1¼ | 2½ |
| 1½ | 3½ |
| 2 | 5 |
| 3 | 6 |
| 4 | 10 |

It is a good idea to plan the locations of fixtures so that most, if not all, can be vented through one stack. For example, figure 1 shows that by locating the bathroom next to the kitchen, it is practical to vent all fixtures in both rooms through the one stack. This consideration should not necessarily dictate overall room arrangement.

## Floor Drains

Floor drains are required in shower stalls, milkrooms, and milking parlors. They are often installed in laundry rooms, basements, and utility rooms.

Floor drains should be trapped. If the building drain is laid under the floor, it must be at a sufficient depth to permit installation of the trap. Floor drains are usually set close enough to the building drain to make separate venting unnecessary.

A floor drain should be flush with the floor, and the floor should slope toward the drain from all directions. The grating of the drain should be removable so the drain can be cleaned.

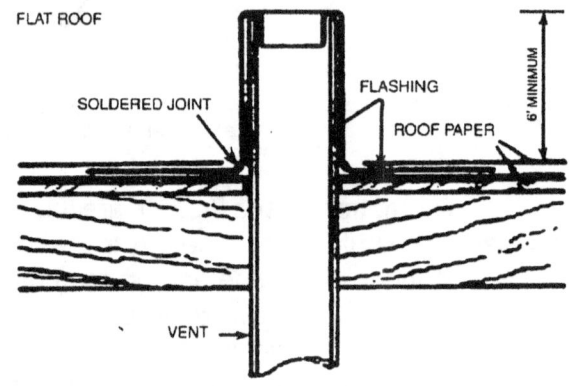

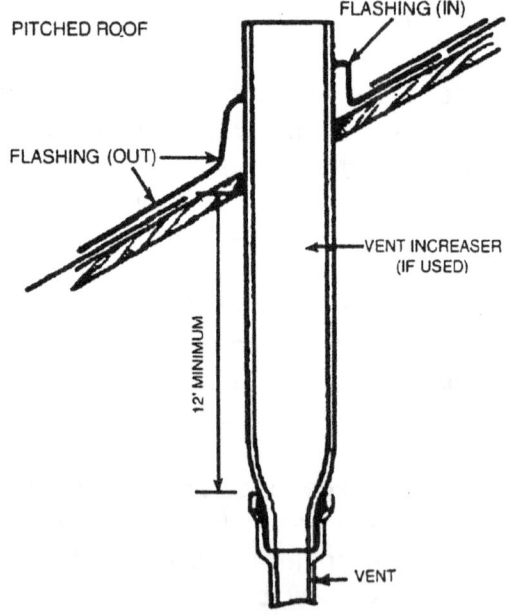

Figure 8 - Installation of roof flashing arround vent stacks.

# PIPE FITTINGS AND CLEANOUTS

### Fittings

If copper tubing is joined directly to galvanized-iron or steel piping, electrolysis will take place under certain conditions and the joint will eventually corrode. Special non-electrical-conducting fittings are available for joining copper tubing to iron or steel piping.

Pipe fittings, such as elbows, tees, nipples, reducers, and couplings, when used with iron or steel pipes, are usually made of the same material as the pipe. Brass fittings are used with brass pipes and copper tubing.

Valves and faucets are usually made of brass or wrought copper. Brass valves made for use with wrought iron, steel, and rigid copper tubing are threaded; those for use with flexible copper tubing are designed for soldering.

Sections of copper tubing and their fittings are joined by soldering. The soldering should be done as follows:

1. Clean the tube end and the cup (inside) of the fitting with steel wool or emery cloth. Remove all loose particles after cleaning. Clean surfaces are essential for good solder connections.
2. Apply a thin coat of flux to the cleaned surfaces of both the tube and the fitting.
3. Assemble the tube and fitting.
4. Apply heat and solder. Heat by directing the flame onto the fitting toward the tube until the solder melts. The solder will flow and fill the joint.
5. Remove excess flux and solder with a small brush or soft cloth while the metal is still hot.
6. Allow the joint to cool, with-out moving it.

Cast-iron drainage pipe sections and fittings are usually of the hub-and-spigot type and are joined by packing with hemp tow or oakum and sealing with lead (fig. 9). The joint must be fitted and packed so that the sections are concentric, leaving no obstructions to the flow of liquid or projections against which solids can lodge. The direction of waste flow must always be as shown in figure 9.

A recently developed system for joining cast-iron drainage, waste, and vent piping requires only a wrench to assemble. The pipe sections are manufactured without the usual hub and spigot ends and are joined by a neoprene sleeve gasket held in place oy a wrap-around stainless steel shield fastened by stainless steel bands with worm-drive clamps (fig. 10). The absence of hubs enables 2- and 3-inch piping to be installed inside standard 2 x 4's. This method of connection may be used both above and below grade.

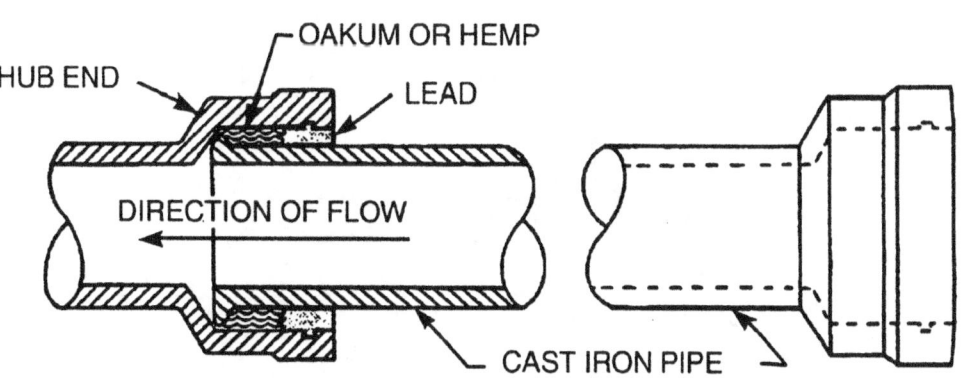

Figure 9 - Bell-and-spigot joint in cast-iron pipe.

Branch drainpipes should be connected to larger drainpipes so that the direction of flow in the system is maintained (see fig. 7).

Where a change in the direction of drainage piping is necessary, sweep bends (fig. 11) should be used whenever possible, because angled turns tend to reduce the rate of flow.

**Cleanouts**

Wastes that will cling to the inside of pipe walls are sometimes discharged into drainage sytems.

Also, when cool, greases congeal and may stick to pipe walls. To permit cleaning of pipes, cleanouts should be provided through which such matter can be removed or dislodged. Cleanouts usually consist of 45-degree Y-fittings with removable plugs (figs. 11 and 12). They should be the same size as the pipe in which they are installed.

Cleanouts should be installed where they are readily accessible and where cleanout tools can be easily inserted into the drainpipe. Place one cleanout at or near the foot of the soil stack (fig. 13). Install others at intervals of not more than 50 feet along horizontal drainage lines that are 4 inches or less in diameter.

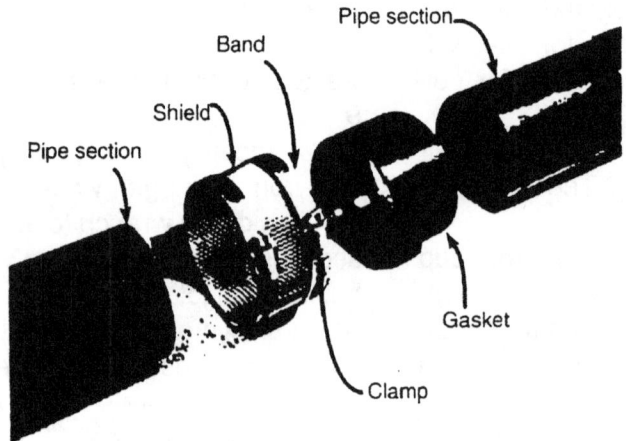

Figure 10 - The newest method of joining pipe is with neoprene gasket shield, and clamps.

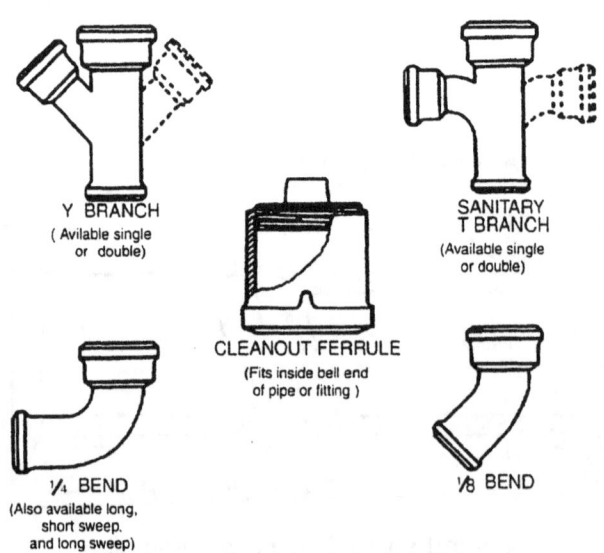

Figure 11 - Common cast-iron soil-pipe fittings.

# 11
# FIXTURES

Many styles of each type of plumbing fixture are available. Selection is mostly a matter of personal preference. The style and size of a fixture should harmonize with the room in which it is installed.

When designing a new house or building, allow enough space for the desired fixtures. When selecting new fixtures for existing buildings, be sure they will fit into the space available. Draw to scale floor plans of the rooms in which fixtures will be installed (for example, 1/4 or 1/2 inch can equal 1 foot). Arrange cardboard cutouts of the fixtures, drawn to the same scale, on the floor plans.

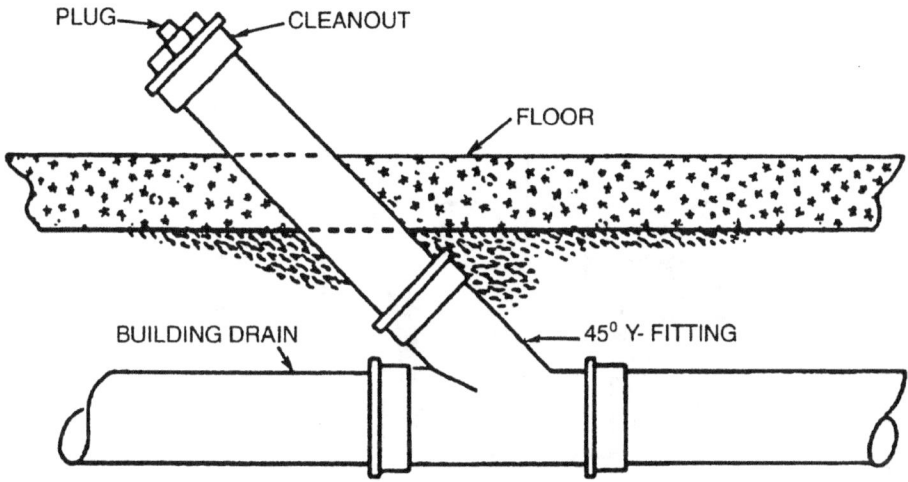

Figure 12 - A 45° Y-fitting and cleanout in building drain.

Manufacturers of plumbing fixtures sometimes have cutouts of their equipment available for planning purposes.

Some plumbing fixtures are supported on the floor alone, some on the wall alone, and some partly on each. Support must be substantial; otherwise a fixture may pull away from the wall and leave a crack. Appropriate carriers or brackets are available for supporting wall-hung fixtures. Guidance on necessary support framing and attachment may be had from fixture manufacturers or dealers.

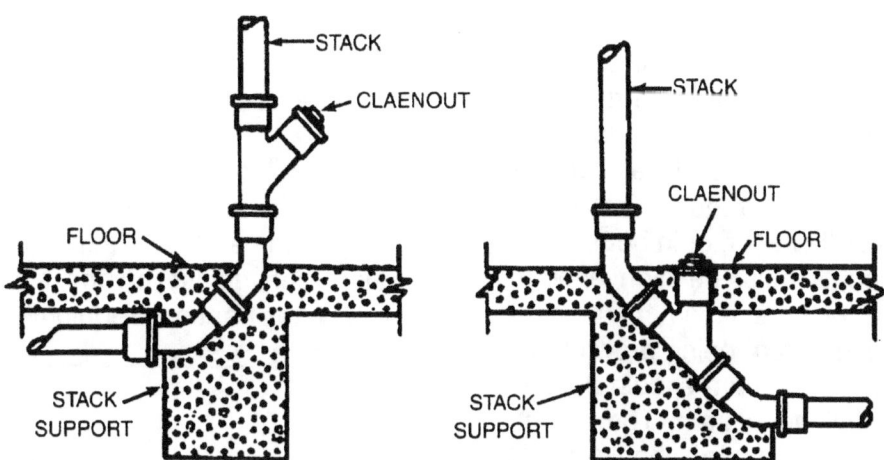

Figure 13 - Soil and waste pipe cleanouts and supports.

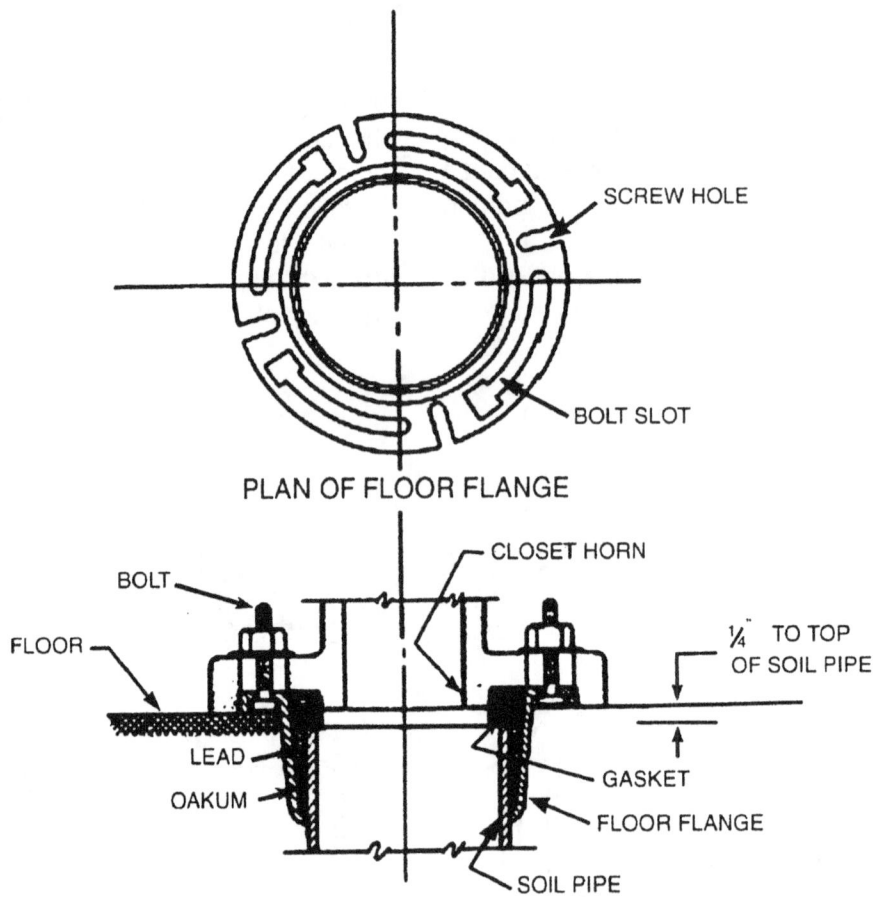

Figure 14 - One method of connecting water closet to the soil pipe.

Water closets are available for either floor or wall mounting. The floor-mounted type bolts to a floor flange, which in turn attaches to the floor (fig. 14) or to the closet bend below. The wall-mounted type is supported by carriers attached to the wall studding or to both the wall and the floor (chair carriers). Six-inch wall studding is recommended if wall-type carriers are used. Tubs are available either for floor support alone or for floor and wall support combined, and may require additional framing in the wall or floor, or in both.

Faucet spouts must be high enough above a lavatory or sink rim to prevent water in the fixture from being drawn back into the faucet if a vacuum should be created in the plumbing system. The height, which is known as "air gap," should be at least twice the diameter of the faucet opening (see fig. 6). Normally it should not be less than 1 inch for lavatories; 1 1/2 inches for sinks, laundry trays, and 3/4-inch bath faucets; and 2 inches for 1-inch bath faucets.

### Water Treatment

Water for domestic use may require treatment to make it suitable. An analysis will determine the treatment required. Dealers can advise on the selection and use of water-treatment equipment.

# Plumbing Check for House Buyers

If you are considering buying a previously occupied house, you should examine and evaluate the condition of the plumbing. The following questions will suggest features that should not be overlooked:

Are there water stains in the building, indicating leaks in the water-supply or drainage piping? If so, have the leaks been corrected satisfactorily?

Is the flow of water from the faucets good and strong, indicating absence of corrosion or scaling in the supply piping? If not, can the deficiency be corrected economically?

Do the fixtures drain quickly and quietly and maintain the water seals in the traps, indicating an adequate vented drainage system? If not, can the deficiency be corrected economically?

Are all fixtures and piping firmly anchored or supported!

Does the water closet flush completely and shut off completely? Does the tank refill quietly? If not, can the deficiency be corrected economically?

Do faucets and valves operate freely and close completely? If not, can the deficiency be corrected economically?

Are the fixtures chipped and stained? Do they need to be replaced?

Do the stoppers hold? If not, can they be readily and cheaply replaced or repaired?

# WATER HEATERS

A house plumbing system usually includes a water heater or a hot-water storage tank if the water is heated in the central heating plant. (Water heaters are also required in milkhouses, see p. 16.)

Electric, gas, and oil-fueled water heaters are available. Each type comes in a wide variety of sizes. Instructions for connecting water heaters to plumbing systems come with the units. The tanks have the necessary internal piping already installed and the only connections required are the hot- and cold-water and fuel lines. Gas- or oil-fired water heaters require flues to vent the products of combustion.

Pressure and temperature relief valves are essential and should be on all water heaters and hot-water storage tanks. Their purpose is to relieve pressure in the tank and pipes if other control equipment fails and the water temperature goes high enough to generate dangerous pressure. As water heats it expands, and the expansion may be enough to rupture the tank or pipes if the water cannot be forced back into the cold-water line or discharged through a relief outlet.

The size of hot-water storage tank needed in the house depends upon the number of persons in the family, the volume of hot water that may be required during peak use periods (for example, during bathing or laundering periods), and the "recovery rate" of the heating unit. Household water heaters are generally available with tanks in a range of sizes from about 30 to 80 gallons.

The "recovery rate" of water heaters varies with the type and capacity of the heating element. In standard conventional models, oil and gas heaters usually have higher recovery rates than electric heaters of similar size. However, a relatively new "quick recovery" type of electric water heater is available. Its two high-wattage heating elements provide hot water at a rapid rate.

For a family of 4 or 5 persons, tank sizes should be about 30 to 40 gallons for oil or gas heaters, 40 gallons for quick-recovery electric heaters, and 40 to 52 gallons for standard electric heaters. For larger families, or where unusually heavy use will be made of hot water, correspondingly larger capacity heaters should be installed. Advice on the size needed may be obtained from Extension home demonstration agents, equipment dealers, and power company representatives. Power suppliers may offer special reduced rates for electric water heating. If "off peak" electric heating will be used, be sure that the tank will hold enough hot water to last from one heating period to the next.

## PROTECTING WATER PIPES FROM FREEZING

If water freezes in a pipe, the pipe may be ruptured or otherwise damaged.

Freezing will not occur if a pipe is well insulated (fig. 15) and the water is allowed to flow continuously. However, insulation does not stop the loss of heat it merely reduces the rate of loss and the water may freeze if it stands in a pipe, even a well-insulated one, for some time in cold weather.

Pipes laid in the ground are usually difficult to insulate effectively because of moisture; insulation must stay dry to be effective. But a pipe laid below the frostline is not likely to freeze even if not insulated.

In areas subject to freezing temperatures, it is advisable not to install water pipes in outside walls of buildings. Should it be necessary to do so, they should be protected from freezing.

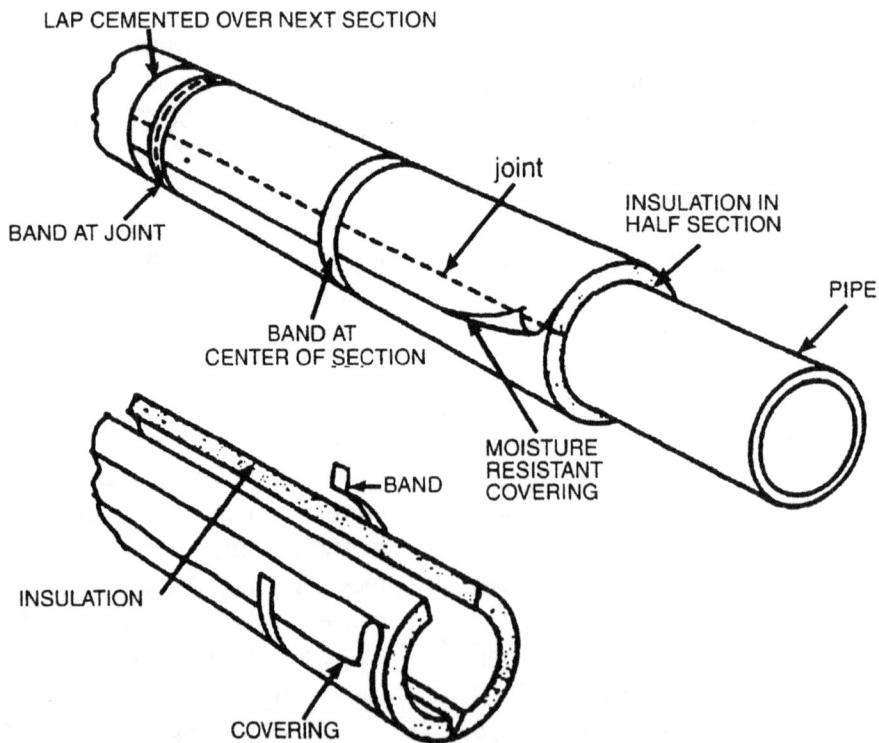

Figure 15 - One method of applying insulation to pipe

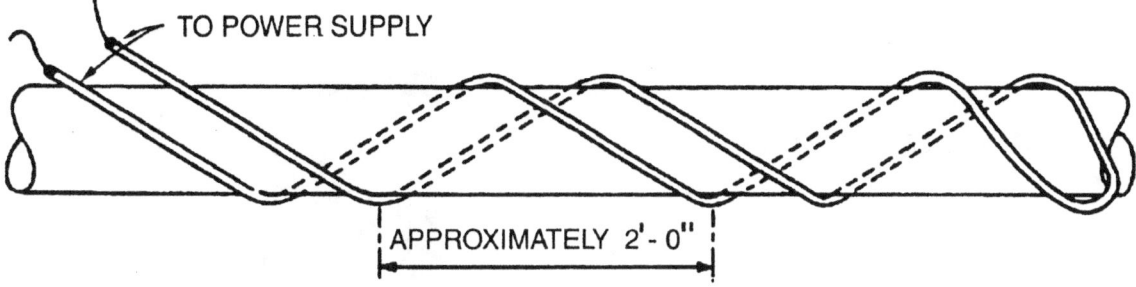

Figure 16 - Application of heating cable to pipe to prevent freezing

Electric heating cable can be used to prevent pipes from freezing. Each unit of cable should be folded at the midpoint and wrapped around the pipe as shown in figure 16. Electric heating cable may also be used to thaw frozen pipe.

## CONDENSATION

In areas where the air gets hot and humid, condensation (sweating) is very likely to occur on pipes carrying cold water. This can be prevented by insulating the pipes. The insulation will also help to keep the water cool. To prevent condensation from collecting in the insulation, it should be covered with a good vapor barrier. Vapor barriers are ordinarily available from the same sources as the insulation.

Condensation may also occur on a water-closet tank in hot, humid weather. This may be prevented by insulating the tank. Insulating jackets, or liners, that fit inside water-closet tanks are available. When installed, they prevent the water from cooling the outer surface of the tank.

## SERVICE-BUILDING PLUMBING

### Water-Supply Piping

Water is needed in all buildings and yards where livestock are kept.

In stall-type dairy barns, water is usually provided by means of water bowls. The bowls must be designed to prevent back siphoning of water into the water-supply piping. This may be done by using valves with outlets above the overflow rim of the bowl (fig. 17).

The supply piping for water bowls is often mounted on the stall frame where it may be subject to freezing. Freezing can be prevented by wrapping heating cable around the pipe, and covering the cable and pipe with insulation (figs. 15 and 16). If the pipe is laid underground, the riser to the bowl must be protected against freezing.

Precautions against back siphoning of water into the supply piping and against freezing must also be taken with troughs and other types of stock waterers. Heating devices are available to prevent freezing.

Where there is danger of the pipes freezing in service buildings, a stop-and-waste valve should be installed between the building service pipe and the distribution piping. The valve, which may be buried in the ground where the service pipe enters the building, will permit draining the piping in the building during cold weather. When the valve handle, which extends above the ground, is closed, the water in the service pipe drains through an opening in the valve

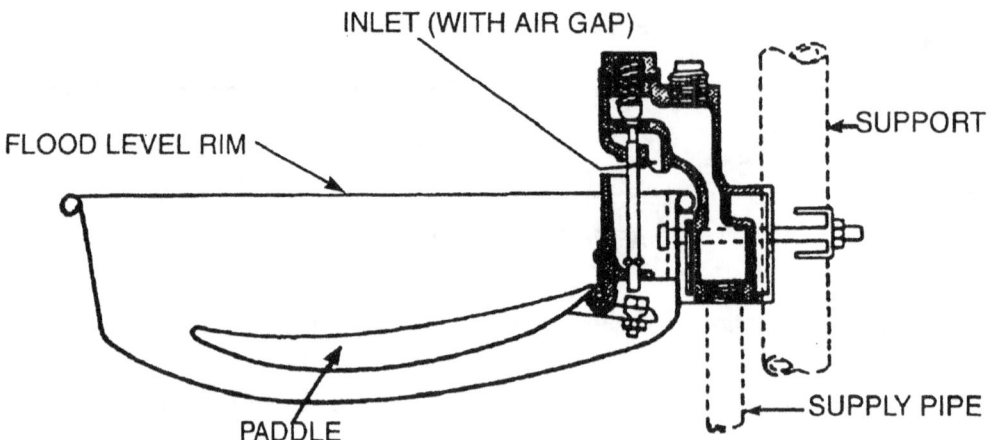

Figure 17 - Livestock watering bowl.

into the ground. If the ground around the valve is not sufficiently porous to absorb the drainage, it should be made so by packing with gravel or broken stone.

In cold climates, outdoor faucets should be the frostproof type. Frostproof hydrants are designed to drain the water left in them when they are turned off. This prevents freezing.

Water is needed for washing down stall barns and milking parlors. Both hot and cold water should be provided in the operator area of milking parlors for washing udders, rinsing pails, and other cleaning.

Hot and cold water are required in the milkhouse or milk room.

**Note: Consult your dairy inspector regarding regulations before installing milkhouse plumbing.** A water heater should be included in the milkhouse plumbing system. Water heaters for the dairy are usually larger than those used for household water heating and may operate at a higher temperature. On large dairy farms where a considerable amount of equipment must be washed and sterilized, a steam boiler may be advisable.

Hose connections or other outlets should be provided for flushing paved livestock feeding and resting areas.

**Drainage Piping**

Proper handling and disposal of dairy building wastes—especially from the gutters in stall barns, in milking parlors, and in milk rooms-is essential to prevent contamination of dairy products. Local health authorities should be consulted when planning a dairy waste-disposal system. All requirements in the milk code must be followed.

Milkhouse drainage systems must be adequate to carry away the waste water from washing utensils, the milk-cooling equipment, and the milkhouse. In small milkhouses, one 4-inch drain may be adequate; in larger ones, two drains may be needed-one under the washing vat and one in the center of the floor. The milkhouse wastes should not drain into the household sewage-disposal system, but into a separate system. Milkhouse drains should be trapped and vented; the method is the same as for house drains.

Your milk code may require a washroom with a lavatory and water closet for use by the dairy help. Wastes from this washroom are sewage and should not drain into the milkhouse or barn waste-disposal systems. Either provide a separate disposal system or, if practical, use the household sewage-disposal system.

# GLOSSARY OF PLUMBING TERMS

## TABLE OF CONTENTS

|  | Page |
|---|---|
| Accepted Standards.....Building Main | 1 |
| Building Sewer.....Dry Vent | 2 |
| Dual Vent.....Indirect Waste Pipe | 3 |
| Interconnection.....Plumbing | 4 |
| Plumbing Fixtures.....Sewage Treatment Plant | 5 |
| Side Vent.....Water Main | 6 |
| Water-Service Pipe.....Yoke Vent | 7 |

# GLOSSARY OF PLUMBING TERMS

## A

**ACCEPTED STANDARDS**
Accepted standards are the standards cited in the manual, or other standards approved by the authority having jurisdiction over plumbing.

**AIR GAP**
The air gap in a water-supply system for plumbing fixture is the vertical distance between the supply-fitting outlet (spout) and the highest possible water level in the receptor when flooded.
If the plane at the end of the spout is at an angle to the surface of the water, the mean gap is the basis for measurement.

**APPROVED**
Approved means accepted as satisfactory to the authority having jurisdiction over plumbing.

**AREA DRAIN**
An area drain is a drain installed to collect surface or rain water from an open area.

## B

**BACKFLOW**
Backflow means the flow of water into a water-supply system for any source except its regular one. Back siphonage is one type of backflow.

**BACKFLOW CONNECTION**
A backflow connection is any arrangement whereby backflow can occur.

**BACK VENT**
A back vent is a branch vent installed primarily for the purpose of protecting fixture traps from self-siphonage.

**BRANCH**
A branch is any part of a piping system other than a main. (See Main.)

**BRANCH INTERVAL**
A branch interval is a length of soil or waste stack corresponding in general to a story height, but in no case less than 8 feet, within which the horizontal branches from one floor or story of the building are connected to the stack.

**BRANCH VENT**
A branch vent is any vent pipe connecting from a branch of the drainage system to the vent stack.

**BUILDING DRAIN**
The building (house) drain is that part of the lowest horizontal piping of a building-drainage system which receives the discharge from soil, waste, and other drainage pipes inside the walls of the building and conveys it to the building (house) sewer beginning 5 feet outside the inner face of the building wall.

**BUILDING-DRAINAGE SYSTEM**
The building-drainage system consists of all piping provided for carrying waste water, sewage, or other drainage from the building to the street sewer or place of disposal.

**BUILDING MAIN**
The building main is the water-supply pipe including fittings and accessories, from the water (street) main or other source of supply to the first branch of the water-distributing system.

**BUILDING SEWER**
   The building (house) sewer is that part of the horizontal piping of a building-drainage system extending from the building drain 5 feet outside of the inner face of the building wall to the street sewer or other place of disposal (a cesspool, septic tank, or other type of sewage-treatment device or devices) and conveying the drainage of but one building site.

**BUILDING SUBDRAIN**
   A building (house) subdrain is that portion of a drainage system which cannot drain by gravity into the building sewer.

## C

**CIRCUIT VENT**
   A circuit vent is a group vent extending from in front of the last fixture connection of a horizontal branch to the vent stack.

**COMBINATION FIXTURE**
   Combination fixture is a trade term designating an integral combination of one sink and one or two laundry trays in one fixture.

**CONTINUOUS-WASTE-AND-VENT**
   A continuous-waste-and-vent is a vent that is a continuation of and in a straight line with the drain to which it connects. A continuous-waste-and-vent is further defined by the angle of the drain and vent at the point of connection make with the horizontal; for example, vertical continuous-waste-and-vent, 45 continuous-waste-and-flat (small angle) continuous-waste-and-vent.

**CONTINUOUS WASTE**
   A waste from two or more fixtures connected to a single trap.

**CROSS-CONNECTION**
   See: INTERCONNECTION

## D

**DEVELOPED LENGTH**
   The developed length of a pipe is its length along the center line of the pipe and fittings.

**DIAMETER**
   Unless specifically stated, the term diameter means the nominal diameter as designated commercially.

**DISTANCE**
   The distance or difference in elevation between two sloping pipes is the distance between the intersection of their center lines with the center line of the pipe to which both are connected.

**DOUBLE OFFSET**
   A double offset is two offsets installed in succession or series in the same line.

**DRAIN**
   A drain or drain pipe is any pipe which carries water or waterborne wastes in a building drainage system.

**DRAINAGE PIPING**
   Drainage piping is all or any part of the drain pipes of a plumbing system.

**DRY VENT**
   A dry vent is any vent that does not carry water or water-borne wastes.

## DUAL VENT
A dual vent (sometimes called a unit vent) is a group vent connecting at the junction of two fixture branches and serving as a back vent for both branches.

## E

## EFFECTIVE OPENING
The effective opening is the minimum cross-sectional area between the end of the supply-fitting outlet (spout) and the inlet to the controlling valve or faucet. The basis of measurement is the diameter of a circle of equal cross-sectional area.
If two or more lines supply one outlet, the effective opening is the sum of the effective openings of the individual lines or the area of the combined outlet, whichever is the smaller.

## F

## FIXTURE BRANCH
A fixture branch is the supply pipe between the fixture and the water-distributing pipe.
## FIXTURE DRAIN
A fixture drain is the drain from the trap of a fixture to the junction of the drain with any other drain pipe.
## FIXTURE UNIT
A fixture unit is a factor so chosen that the load-producing values of the different plumbing fixtures can be expressed approximately as multiples of that factor.
## FLOOD LEVEL
Flood level in reference to a plumbing fixture is the level at which water begins to overflow the top or rim of the fixture.

## G

## GRADE
The grade of a line of pipe is its slope in reference to a horizontal plane. In plumbing it is usually expressed as the fall in inches per foot length of pipe.
## GROUP VENT
A group vent is a branch vent that performs its functions for two or more traps.

## H

## HORIZONTAL BRANCH
A horizontal branch is a branch drain extending laterally from a soil or waste stack or building drain, with or without vertical sections or branches, which receives the discharge from one or more fixture drains and conducts it to the soil or waste stack or the building (house) drain.

## I

## INDIRECT WASTE PIPE
An indirect waste pipe is a waste pipe which does not connect directly with the building drainage system, but discharges into it through a properly trapped fixture or receptacle.

### INTERCONNECTION

An interconnection, as the term is used is any physical connection or arrangement of pipes between two otherwise separate building water-supply systems whereby water may flow from one system to the other, the direction of flow depending upon the pressure differential between the two systems.

Where such connection occurs between the sources of two such systems and the first branch from either, whether inside or outside the building, the term cross-connection (American Water Works terminology) applies and is generally used.

## J

### JUMPOVER
See: RETURN OFFSET.

## L

### LEADER
A leader or downspout is the water conductor from the roof to the storm drain or other means of disposal.

### LOOP VENT
A loop vent is the same as a circuit vent except that it loops back and connects with a soil- or waste-stack vent instead of the vent stack.

## M

### MAIN
The main of any system of continuous piping is the principal artery of the system to which branches may be connected.

### MAIN VENT
See: VENT STACK.

## N

### NONPRESSURE DRAINAGE
Nonpressure drainage refers to a condition in which a static pressure cannot be imposed safely on the building drain. This condition is sometimes referred to as gravity flow and implies that the sloping pipes are not completely filled.

## O

### OFFSET
An offset in a line of piping is a combination of elbows or bends which brings one section of the pipe out of line with but into a line parallel with another section.

## P

### PLUMBING
Plumbing is the work or business of installing in buildings the pipes, fixtures, and other apparatus for bringing in the water supply and removing liquid and water-borne wastes. The term is also used to denote the installed fixtures and piping of a building.

## PLUMBING FIXTURES
Plumbing fixtures are receptacles which receive and discharge water, liquid, or water-borne wastes into a drainage system with which they are connected.

## PLUMBING SYSTEM
The plumbing system of a building includes the water-supply distributing pipes; the fixtures and fixture traps; the soil, waste, and vent pipes; the building (house) drain and building (house) sewer; and the storm-drainage pipes; with their devices, appurtenances, and connections all within or adjacent to the building.

## POOL
A pool is a water receptacle used for swimming or as a plunge or other bath, designed to accommodate more than one bather at a time.

## PRESSURE DRAINAGE
Pressure drainage, as used in the manual, refers to a condition in which a static pressure may be imposed safely on the entrances of sloping building drains through soil and waste stacks connected thereto.

## PRIMARY BRANCH
A primary branch of the building (house) drain is the single sloping drain from the base of a soil or waste stack to its junction with the main building drain or with another branch thereof.

## R

## RELIEF VENT
A relief vent is a branch from the vent stack, connected to a horizontal branch between the first fixture branch and the soil or waste stack, whose primary function is to provide for circulation of air between the vent stack and the solid or waste stack.

## RETURN OFFSET
A return offset or jumpover is a double offset installed so as to return the pipe to its original line.

## RISER
A riser is a water-supply pipe which extends vertically one full story or more to convey water to branches or fixtures.

## S

## SAND INTERCEPTOR (SAND TRAP)
A sand interceptor (sand trap) is a water tight receptacle designed and constructed to intercept and prevent the passage of sand or other solids into the drainage system to which it is directly or indirectly connected.

## SANITARY SEWER
A sanitary sewer is a sewer designed or used only for conveying liquid or water-borne waste from plumbing fixtures.

## SECONDARY BRANCH
A secondary branch of the building drain is any branch of the building drain other than a primary branch.

## SEWAGE-TREATMENT PLANT
A sewage-treatment plant consists of structures and appurtenances which receive the discharge of a sanitary drainage system, designed to bring about a reduction in the organic and bacterial content of the waste so as to render it less offensive or dangerous, including septic tanks and cesspools.

## SIDE VENT
A side vent is a vent connecting to the drain pipe through a 45° wye.

## SIZE OF PIPE AND TUBING
The size of pipe and tubing, unless otherwise stated, is the nominal size by which the pipe or tubing is commercially designated. Actual dimensions of the different kinds of pipe and tubing are given in the specifications applying.

## SOIL PIPE
A soil pipe is any pipe which conveys the discharge of water closets or fixtures having similar functions, with or without the discharges from other fixtures.

## STACK
Stack is a general term for the vertical main of a system of soil, waste, or vent piping.

## STACK-VENT
A stack-vent is the extension of a soil or waste stack above the highest horizontal or fixture branch connected to the stack.

## STORM DRAIN
A storm drain is a drain used for conveying rain water, subsurface water, condensate, cooling water, or other similar discharges.

## STORM SEWER
A storm sewer is a sewer used for conveying rain water, subsurface water, condensate, cooling water, or other similar discharges.

## SUBSOIL DRAIN
A subsoil drain is a drain installed for collecting subsurface or seepage water and conveying it to a place of disposal.

## T

## TRAP
A trap is a fitting or device so designed and constructed as to provide a liquid trap seal which will prevent the passage of air through it.

## TRAP SEAL
The trap seal is the vertical distance between the crown weir and the dip of the trap.

## V

## VENT
A vent is a pipe installed to provide a flow of air to or from a drainage system or to provide a circulation of air within such system to protect trap seals from siphonage and back pressure.

## VENT STACK
A vent stack, sometimes called a main vent, is a vertical vent pipe installed primarily for the purpose of providing circulation of air to or from any part of the building-drainage system.

## W

## WASTE PIPE
A waste pipe is a drain pipe which receives the discharge of any fixture other than water closets or other fixtures receiving human excreta.

## WATER MAIN
The water (street) main is a water-supply pipe for public or community use.

WATER-SERVICE PIPE
   The water-service pipe is that part of a building main installed by or under the jurisdiction of a water department or company.

WATER-SUPPLY SYSTEM
   The water-supply system of a building consists of the water-service pipe, the water-distributing pipes, and the necessary connecting pipes, fittings, and control valves.

WET VENT
   A wet vent is a soil or waste pipe that serves also as a vent.

## Y

YOKE VENT
   A yoke vent is a vertical of 45° relief vent of the continuous-waste-and-vent type formed by the extension of an upright wye-branch or 45° wye-branch inlet of the horizontal branch to the stack. It becomes a dual yoke vent when two horizontal branches are thus vented by the same relief vent.

www.ingramcontent.com/pod-product-compliance
Lightning Source LLC
Chambersburg PA
CBHW082210300426
44117CB00016B/2746